GOD SAYS

HELLO
MY NAME IS

Hello, God says my name is

Copyright © 2020 by Dustin Barker

ISBN: 978-1-7350252-0-9

TABLE OF CONTENTS

PREFACE

This book is all about you. I spent many hours on my computer thinking about how the words on these pages would affect your life. I read and re-read through each day diligently asking myself if the words would clearly explain the simple truths that I was trying to share. My goal is to make the things that God tells me to share as SIMPLE and CLEAR as possible. One of my passions is for Believers to learn two things, who God is and who God says they are. Through these pages, I hope you walk away with an understanding of who God sees when He looks at you.

So, how did this book end up in your hands? Well, God told me to write this in 2017. I started the first chapter in February 2018 and I finished my writing at the end of 2019. In just a couple of months, I worked through edits to finish in early 2020. Through months of very slow progress and procrastination, here we are, a dream in my heart is now a book in your hands.

I want to add one challenge for you. What is the dream that God has put in your heart? Stop procrastinating! There are people on the other side of your obedience and they are missing out on what you have to offer if you don't say "YES!" So, get started!

I know that a transformed life comes from a renewed mind (Romans 12:2). I am believing that after 31 days you are going to see yourself like never before!

Dustin Barker

INTRODUCTION

Where do you stand with God?

If you aren't sure, then this book could be confusing for you. You see, this book was written to Christians, also known as Believers. To make this very plain and simple, a Believer is someone who identifies with Christ and acknowledges Jesus Christ as their personal Lord and Savior. A Christian identifies with Jesus being the only way to God the Father and that Jesus came and took our sins and mistakes on Himself so we didn't have to pay the price of eternal separation from God.

So, where do you stand with God? Where do you stand with Jesus?

If you still aren't sure, keep reading. The Bible tells us that we have all sinned (Romans 3). Every one of us has made mistakes and walked away from God at one time. The bad news is that God cannot be in a relationship with a sinful being, so our sins separate us from God. The good news is that Jesus paid the price for your sins by dying in your place. The Bible tells us it's very simple to be made right in the eyes of God and we will be brought into God's family by simply believing in Jesus and calling upon His name to save us (Romans 10).

Have you done this? Have you ever called upon the name of Jesus to bring you into right relationship with God? If not, before we move on, let's do it now. Once you do this, then all of these chapters will be about you.

Let's call upon the name of Jesus, pray this out loud:

"Heavenly Father, You said if I would simply call upon the name of Jesus then You would save me. Right now, I invite Jesus into my life. I believe Jesus died for my sins and was raised to life again. I give You my life, thank You for saving me. Amen."

It's that simple, you are now God's child! Now you need to find out everything God says about you.

Why do you need to know who you are?

The first generation of Israel that came out of Egypt missed out on something God had for them because of how they saw themselves. God brought them out of Egypt and was getting ready to bring them into the Promised Land. Israel was re-peatedly told by God that He wanted them to have the land and that they were well able to take it. However, the first gen-eration of Israel to come out of Egypt saw themselves as grasshoppers (Numbers 13:33). God saw able and they saw unable, so they missed out on the Promised Land because they didn't see themselves as God did.

Here is one more story for you. A man named Gideon was found hiding from the enemy in the book of Judges chapter 6. God came to Gideon and said, "You are a mighty warrior." Gideon was fearful and hiding but God saw a warrior. Gideon was small is his eyes but a warrior in God's.

God often sees something different in us than what we see in the mirror. It is time you start seeing yourself how God sees you.

Lastly, before we get started, here is what you can expect.

Each day is going to start with daily scriptures to read. After that, you will get teaching in devotional style to help open up the scriptures and show you how they can apply to you. This is followed by declarations that will be releasing the power that is in your words (Proverbs 18:21) in agreement with what God says. Each reading for the day will then be concluded with a short prayer.

I sincerely hope this book changes how you see you!

DAY 1 Hello, God says my name is

Righteous

"God made him who had no sin to be sin for us, so that in him we might become the righteousness of God."

- 2 Corinthians 5:21 NIV

"No weapon formed against you shall prosper, and every tongue which rises against you in judgment You shall condemn. This is the heritage of the servants of the Lord, and their righteousness is from Me," Says the Lord.

- Isaiah 54:17 NKJV

I thought it would be beneficial to start the first day of this devotional with what I believe is the most important realization of how God sees you now that you are in Christ. In my opinion, learning that you are righteous in God's eyes will help you tremendously as it is essential in the Christian faith to learn this principle.

Have you ever heard the following phrases?

"We are all just sinners."
"I'm just a sinner saved by grace."

I am going to guess that you have probably heard these a time or two.

If you are a born-again Christian and you have given your life to Jesus, then you need to take phrases like these out of your vocabulary IMMEDIATELY. Never allow yourself to say these again. I know that calling yourself a sinner may sound right, but that doesn't make it the truth.

So, are we all sinners? Are we sinners saved by grace? Let's examine this.

Does the Bible say that all of us have sinned? Absolutely it does! We have all sinned and made mistakes. However, just because you HAVE sinned does not make you a sinner ANY-MORE. I know your wheels may be turning and you might be wondering, "Dustin, if I have sinned, doesn't that make me a sinner?" That is a great question! I believe the next couple of pages will help you understand what I am trying to say.

First, you must understand there is a difference between NA-TURE and ACTIONS.

You are a human, right? As a human, let's say you get down on your hands and knees and you start barking like a dog. Are you now a dog? The answer is no. It doesn't matter how many times you bark, you will never be a dog. You could act like a dog for the next week, and guess what, you still wouldn't be a dog. Even if you crawled on your hands and knees for a year and ate nothing but dog food you still would not be a dog. No matter what you do, you could not be a dog. Pay attention to this: just because you act like a dog does not make you a dog. You are a human, it is your nature; you were just acting like a dog.

Your ACTIONS do not change your NATURE and your identity.

How does this illustration apply? If you have called upon the name of Jesus to save you, at that moment you became righteous. God traded your sinful nature for His righteousness. Jesus took on your sin so that He could give you His righteousness (2 Corinthians 5:21). When you called upon the name of Jesus you were given a righteous nature.

Now that you are a Christian, when you sin, it doesn't make you a sinner because your nature is righteous. It's the same as acting like a dog doesn't make you a dog because you are a human. If you sin, your actions are like a sinner, but your nature is still righteous.

Before we go any further, let me briefly explain righteousness. Righteous can simply be stated as right in the eyes of God. Righteousness is the holiness and perfection of God Himself. To make it very plain and simple, righteousness is the complete opposite of sin.

So, are we sinners saved by grace?

No, the TRUTH is, if you belong to Jesus, you WERE a sinner, but now you are saved by grace. You need to see yourself as God sees you. You cannot be righteous and unrighteous (a sinner) at the same time. This would be like a light being on and off at the same time. It's not possible. You are either one or the other.

You WERE once a sinner who couldn't make yourself righteous and acting righteously wouldn't make you righteous. Even if you gave to the poor, prayed, went to church, and followed the ten commandments you could never change who you were: a sinner. Your actions couldn't change your nature.

Righteousness is a gift from God (Romans 5:17). Our actions could not earn it. 2 Corinthians 5:21 in the NIV says that "God made him who had no sin to be sin for us, so that in him we might become the righteousness of God." Jesus was made to be sin so that God could make you righteous. The Bible even tells us that God gave us His very own righteousness (Isaiah 54:17).

Just to be clear I am not saying that we do not sin. I am saying that our ACTIONS do not determine our NATURE. Jesus took away your sinful nature and gave you His righteousness. God no longer sees a sinner.

I believe that if you continue to call yourself a sinner it devalues the high price that Jesus paid for you. Jesus didn't take your sin to leave you a sinner. You are no longer a sinner, you are a child of God. You can act like a dog, but it doesn't make you a dog.

Some of the toughest times to believe this is right when you make mistakes. It is in these moments where you need to stand up and say "I am the righteousness of God in Christ Jesus," even when you don't feel like it.

Satan wants you to be sin-conscious so you won't come boldly to the throne of grace. When we are sin-conscious we hide from God just like Adam did in the garden. But, when we are righteousness-conscious we will come to God boldly, unafraid, and unashamed.

As you stand before God, He sees righteousness.

And if God calls you righteous, then how dare you call yourself a sinner?

Declare who God says you are today!

God says my name is Righteous

I am right with God

God sees me as innocent and blameless

I am the righteousness of God in Christ Jesus

I'm no longer a sinner, I am saved

_____

Today's Prayer:

Heavenly Father,

Thank You for giving me Your righteousness. Help me to see myself as You see me. When I sin or mess up, show me that I can still come to You boldly because You see righteousness even when I don't. I believe that I am no longer a sinner because in Jesus I have been made brand new. Thank You for making me innocent and blameless in Your sight. Today, I choose to believe that I am righteous, therefore I can come boldly to Your throne as if I had never sinned.

Amen.

Called

"The one who calls you is faithful, and he will do it."

- 1 Thessalonians 5:24 NIV

"I pray that the eyes of your heart may be enlightened in order that you may know the hope to which he has called you, the riches of his glorious inheritance in his holy people, and his incomparably great power for us who believe."

- Ephesians 1:18-19a NIV

Today your name is Called. It's easy to look at preachers like Billy Graham and see that God had called them, but many people do not think the same of themselves. Sometimes it's easy for us to see the call on someone else's life, but it's not as easy to see the call for ourselves. There are also still many that only associate the word "called" with someone that is in ministry, however, the reality is that God has called all of us.

There are two meanings to the word "called" that I would like to discuss. The first meaning is similar to the word "invite." To better understand what this looks like, take a moment, and imagine with me that the White House is throwing a fancy dinner party. News about this party travels fast and you find out that they are serving your favorite meal that night. Well, when you hear about it, you decide you are going to head over to the White House and join them. However, once you arrive, you run into a problem, because you quickly realize that security won't let you on the property. Do you know why? You were not invited. No one called you to come. It doesn't matter how much you want to join the dinner party. Without a call, you are on the outside looking in.

In a very similar way, we were on the outside looking into God's family and God's plan. There was no getting in simply because we wanted to; we had to first be invited or called. This is what Jesus was saying in John 15:16a (NIV), "You did not choose me, but I chose you." God called us, He invited us, and He summoned us to be a part of all He is doing. He specifically sent an invite to you because He wanted you to be included.

I want you to know this: NOBODY can sneak into God's family. God doesn't look at you and wonder, "How did you get in here?" You didn't have to sneak in while God wasn't looking! He SPECIFICALLY and INTENTIONALLY called you and sent you an invitation to be included.

Another meaning of "called" is to be divinely selected by God for a special purpose. This is typically what people mean when they say someone has a "call" on their life. I believe we often limit the meaning of this word only to people who are "called" to full-time ministry. However, we are all called to a special purpose. There is no one else on the planet that can be you. No one else can do exactly what you do. You must realize that you came to Earth with an assignment and are gifted uniquely. You are wired like no one else and there is not another person that has the same combination of talents and gifts that you do. God knew the world needed you so He gifted you and called you for a special purpose to reach the people in your life.

You see, ultimately we are "called" to people. That is God's end game. People are His treasure and your purpose in life is to help God reach them. There are people in your life that I may never meet. You will have neighbors, friends, and family that I could never reach. You have skills that I do not have and those skills put you in positions (that I could never be in) to reach people (that may never listen to me). YOU ARE CALLED TO PEOPLE!

You are a city on a hill. You are the light of the world (Matthew 5:14). Not only has God called you into His family, but you have a call to change the world around you. Stop letting the enemy lie to you and say you aren't important. Stop letting the enemy tell you it's the job of pastors and evangelists to reach people. IT'S YOUR JOB. You are called to reach the world around you. You have a sphere of influence (neighbors, family, friends, and co-workers) that is different than every other person on the planet. You are uniquely gifted and talented to reach those that others couldn't.

Start noticing that you work for more than just a paycheck; you are there for people. Your neighbors may have been directed by God to move in next to you because you were their only hope to hear about Jesus. Lives are on the line. God has people for you to reach everywhere you go. Don't overlook which gym you go to and where you get your hair cut, those people need you because God is with you.

Everywhere you are, you are on assignment because you are CALLED. God is looking for help to reach the people of this planet. God NEEDS you! He has CALLED you!

Declare who God says you are today!

God says my name is Called

I was invited into God's family

I am chosen and selected

I have the call of God on my life

God has called me to be a part of His plan to reach people

Today's Prayer:

Heavenly Father,

I believe that I am called. Thank You for inviting me to be a part of Your family and to be a part of Your team. I ask that You would reveal to me what my purpose and place is in Your Kingdom. Show me what You created and CALLED me to do while I am still on this Earth. You called me long before I ever called upon You. I believe I have value so today I choose to stop comparing myself to others and choose to believe that I am called by God for a specific purpose.

Amen.

DAY 3   Hello, God says my name is

Child of God

"Behold what manner of love the Father has bestowed on us, that we should be called children of God!"

-     1 John 3:1a NKJV

"Therefore you are no longer a slave but a son, and if a son, then an heir of God through Christ."

-     Galatians 4:7 NKJV

The Bible tells us that when you receive Jesus Christ as your Lord and Savior, a transaction takes place. Before Christ, you were once in darkness. You were a part of the kingdom of darkness. But good news, it doesn't stop there, when you called upon the name of Jesus you were then translated into God's Kingdom (Colossians 1:13). Part of this transaction is that you are now adopted into God's family. Galatians 4:7 says you are no longer a slave, but a son (or daughter). You are God's child now! This is not a future moment; this transaction already took place the moment you received Jesus (John 1:12).

Do you remember the days back when you were just a kid on the playground? Had you ever heard the phrase, "Well, my dad could beat up your dad?" It's funny to think that children don't know any better and will often assume their dad could beat up anyone they put in front of them. Have you ever seen a child hide behind their dad's legs? Often when children are afraid they will hold tightly to their father's leg and hide. Children can often do this when they are around a dog that they are unsure of or people they have never met. To a child, a dad can feel like a protective shield that they use so nothing can harm them.

Children often have this innate sense of confidence when they are around their father. As children of God, how much more confidence should we have in our Heavenly Father? Our confidence in God should be greater than a child's confidence in an earthly dad.

Take a moment and imagine a child that sees a dog that terrifies them. The dog stares down the young child as their dad walks over. When the dad gets to the little child, they quickly hide behind his leg. At that moment the child is comforted by the fact that they are protected by their father. Just moments before they were frightened, but now imagine they are yelling at the dog saying, "Yeah, you better not come over here!" Their fear left because their dad is there and he will protect them and take care of the problem.

Well, our Heavenly Father is the biggest and toughest around, nobody can hang with Him. Think about this: The Creator of all the Universe calls you His child. When battles or problems arise, have confidence in knowing that your Dad, the God of the Universe, watches over you, and will fight for you. You have no reason to be afraid of the devil. You have no reason to be afraid of the troubles of life. When fear speaks loudly, your Father is with you. When problems scream out to you, simply hide behind your Heavenly Father and yell back at those problems and say, "Yeah, what are you going to do now?"

As a Father, God is a safe place to hide. Psalm 91:4 says, "He shall cover you with His feathers, and under His wings you shall take refuge." Friend, you are God's child. You are ALREADY in the family! There is no earning your way in and God doesn't make you sit out on the porch if you're naughty or disobedient. Right now, you are just as much God's beloved child as you will ever be. Rest under His shadow knowing God will silence your enemies.

Not only do fathers provide protection, but their children get special privileges. When I was growing up I never had to beg my parents to come into the house. If I wanted a glass of water, I just took it. Whenever I wanted something to eat I would just go into the refrigerator and take whatever looked good. This is how God wants us to approach Him. That might sound arrogant to you but it's not arrogance, it is confidence in His goodness.

You see, you can come boldly to God, not because of how good you've been, but **because of how good He is**. He delights when you come boldly. Religion has taught us to beg and the reason we beg is because we think we need to twist God's arm to get something. However, God's hand is open and He gives to His children freely. For this reason, we do not need to beg, but just take what is being offered!

You are in the family! God's hand is open, so freely take what He is giving.

Declare who God says you are today!

God says my name is Child of God

My Father protects me from evil

I am a child of the Creator of the universe

I am in the family of God

I am a beloved child of God with special privileges

Today's Prayer:

Heavenly Father,

I believe I am Your child. I believe that You are a good Father to me. I was once lost, but You have adopted me into Your family. Thank You for bringing me in and loving me. Help me to see what it means to be in Your family and what it means to be Your child. I believe there is protection in Your presence and I am unafraid to come boldly to You.

Amen.

DAY 4 Hello, God says my name is

Loved

"We love because he first loved us."

- 1 John 4:19 NIV

"As the Father has loved me, so have I loved you. Now remain in my love."

- John 15:9 NIV

Pretend with me for a minute that you have a son. When he was born you decided to name him John. Now, if your last name is Williams, what would be your son's name? John Williams. You got it! When John goes to kindergarten for his first day and stands in front of the class, he is going to say "Hi, my name is… John Williams," of course. Let's take this a little further. Imagine John is misbehaving. Now, what is his name? Well, it is still John Williams. Even if John makes mistakes, his identity stays the same. What if John acts like a Bruce someday? This does not matter because John's actions can't change his identity.

What am I trying to prove? Well, I want you to see that this boy does not get his identity from how he acts. The child simply gets his identity from what his parents wanted to name him. In the same way, God has chosen to name you loved. How you act does not change this. You are loved, it's your identity. Your actions cannot change the fact that when God looks at you all He sees is loved.

If your son, John Williams, comes home someday after school and says "I don't 'feel' like John Williams anymore," that will not change that he is, in fact, John Williams. John could look in the mirror every day and say "I am not John," but would that change the fact that his parents still look at him and see John?

You see, it doesn't matter how you feel. You are loved. Your feelings will lie to you. Satan wants you to live by your feelings. You could look in the mirror and see unloveable, but God sees who you really are, loved. Many people all over the planet still look at themselves and question if God loves them, but that doesn't change what He sees when He looks at us. He sees loved.

God has decided to call you loved regardless of how you act or look. This is your name even if you feel unloved. Loved is who you are even when you mess up. There is no mistake you could make that could change this.

God made the choice that He loved you before you took your first breath. There is ABSOLUTELY NOTHING you could do that would ever make God say you are not loved. Maybe you have heard "God loves you" ten thousand times, but it will still benefit you to meditate on this fact today. God loves you. He is on your team. Your identity is, and always will be, loved.

You can hear "God loves you" for years and still fall into a wrong belief that God loves us only when we are behaving properly or being obedient. Please remember that God sent His Son to die for you, because He loved you, long before you ever chose to love Him. Some Christians have no trouble looking at someone who isn't right with God and telling them how much God loves them, but they fail to believe it when they look in the mirror. Other times we may think God loves us only when we are actively pursuing Him and when we are loving Him. However, the truth found in 1 John 4:19 NIV says "We love because he first loved us." This means that the only reason we even have the ability to love is because God loved us first. So, before you could even make the choice if you wanted to be loved or not, God chose to love you.

Loved is such a beautiful name to be called. Think about it, as humans, why do we desire close friendships? Why do people date? Why do so many people get married? It's because people long to be loved. At the core of every relationship, people are looking for someone to love them. Within love, there is a security that someone else cares about your well-being.

The love of God was never meant to be a cliché that was thrown on billboards and bumper stickers. The way God looks at you compares with nothing else. How does a man look at his bride as she walks down the aisle toward him? Even the strongest men have trouble controlling their emotions, but this doesn't even compare to the passion that burns in God's eyes for you.

To help us picture this, I would like you to take a moment and think about how a parent looks at their child when they see them for the first time. If you are already a parent, then hopefully this is a little easier for you. If you haven't had children yet, take some time today and ask a friend who is a parent what it was like the first time they looked at their first child. How much love wells up inside a parent when they lay their eyes on that child? Do you think it's at all possible for that child to make their parents mad that day? Is there anything that a newborn could do to make their parents say "We don't love you" the day they are born? When that baby makes a mess in their diaper, does that change the mother's love? Absolutely not.

This is no different with God. When you make messes it doesn't make you unlovable. He looks at you every day as if it were the first time He saw you. And on top of that, human love in a parent doesn't compare to the capacity God has to love you.

What am I hoping you will get today? I want you to realize that God loves you like nothing else. You may already believe this but it's bigger and deeper than you know. The Bible says He rejoices over you with singing (Zephaniah 3:17). God sings over you because the thought of you excites Him that much.

Just the thought of you brings a smile to God's face.

Declare who God says you are today!

God says my name is Loved

I am God's beloved

God loves me

I am the apple of God's eye

God rejoices over me with singing

Today's Prayer:

Heavenly Father,

I am asking that You would reveal Your love to me all over again. I believe You love me, but I want to walk in a greater understanding of that love. Show me how much I mean to You. I want to walk in greater confidence knowing that I bring a smile to Your face. Thank You for loving me before I ever loved You.

Amen.

DAY 5

Protected

"A thousand may fall dead beside you, ten thousand all around you, but you will not be harmed."

- Psalm 91:7 NLT

"and so no disaster will strike you, no violence will come near your home."

- Psalm 91:10 GNT

"God will put his angels in charge of you to protect you wherever you go."

- Psalm 91:11 GNT

Here is today's challenge: make God's word very simple. Why do I say that? People can sometimes read the Bible and hear God's promises and then say things like, "I know the Bible says that but..."

So, what do I mean by making things simple? I mean, whatever God says, let it mean exactly what it says, no matter what you have seen, heard, or experienced.

Imagine I come to you and say, "I'm going to mow your lawn tomorrow." This would be a very simple promise. It's rather difficult to make this confusing. Would you need to look at me and ask "What do you mean by that?" No, because I told you exactly what I was going to do.

How do you make my simple promise confusing? You start asking questions like, "Did Dustin really mean what he said?" or "What if he doesn't come to mow tomorrow?" You could look at your neighbor's yard and say, "Our neighbors forgot to mow their yard, maybe Dustin will forget to mow our yard."

You have a decision to make: do you take me at my word and believe me or do you pick my promise apart and question it? You have to decide if I am a liar or if you will trust my promise. You must decide if I have the integrity to stand by my word.

When God makes promises, you must decide if He is trustworthy and if He has the integrity to fulfill what He said.

Here is what I am trying to show you: for far too long God has made simple promises, and because we don't keep them simple, we don't see what He promised. Do you know why? Jesus said in Matthew 8:13 that things would be done for you as YOU believe. Basically, what He is saying is, whatever you believe, that is what is going to happen. Jesus often inferred that what a person believes is the key factor in what happens. Many times, He looked at people and said it is done for you according to your faith (belief).

So, what do you believe? Do you believe in the simplicity of God's promises of protection? Or do you let Satan's lies and what happens around you distract you? Bad things have happened to people, that is true, but does that change what God promised? When you read Psalm 91 and hear that disaster and violence will not come near you and thousands may fall dead around you but you will not be harmed, do you REALLY believe that? Satan is subtle, he comes to you and says, "God didn't really mean that," and "Sometimes bad things happen to people; there is no controlling that," or "God may let things happen to you sometimes, you don't always get to be protected." Another example of what Satan may tell people is, "Look at so and so, they loved God (probably more than you) and they believed what you do, look what happened to them."

To be honest, you never really know what a person believes. They can tell you what they believe, but God knows what is in their heart. Also, you are not responsible for what anyone else believes; that is between them and God.

Here is what I want to finish with. YOU. ARE. PROTECTED. Psalm 91:4 makes the connection that God will hide you under His feathers like a hen would hide their chicks. And verses 7-11 show very clearly that God doesn't want you to be harmed and no matter what is around you, He doesn't want to let it touch you. Psalm 34:7 also says that God's angels will camp around you and deliver you from whatever comes your way.

Another Bible story that can give you a picture of God's protection in your life is found in Daniel 3. Three Hebrew boys wouldn't bow before another king and because they didn't bow the king threw them in a fire. The fire was so hot that when they were thrown in, the soldiers that threw them in died. However, when the Hebrews came out of the fire (Daniel 3:27), we are told that not a hair was burnt and you couldn't even smell fire on them.

That same protection is available for you. God longs to protect you from any evil that could be thrown your way. Will you believe it? YOU. ARE. PROTECTED. Nothing evil can touch you. God says, "A thousand may fall dead beside you and ten thousand all around you, but you will not be harmed" (Psalm 91:7 NLT). God says, "No disaster will strike you, no violence will come near your home." God also says, "I will put My angels in charge of you to protect you wherever you go." (Psalm 91:7 & 10-11 GNT).

God can be trusted. His Word is good. Satan is subtle and he wants you to question God's Promises. When you hear anything that contradicts the Word, reject it immediately. God WILL protect you from every evil.

YOU. ARE. PROTECTED.

Declare who God says you are today!

God says my name is Protected

A thousand may fall at my side and ten thousand at my right hand, but it won't come near me

I am far from disaster and violence

No evil will overtake me

God protects me everywhere I go

Today's prayer:

Heavenly Father,

Thank You for giving Your angels charge over me to protect me everywhere I go. Open my eyes to see the protection all around me in the moments where I don't feel it. I believe that You are my Shelter, my Protector, and my Defender. Today, I choose to cast all my cares over on You and rest in Your love for me.

Amen.

DAY 6   Hello, God says my name is

Forgiven

"And you, being dead in your trespasses and the uncircumcision of your flesh, He has made alive together with Him, having forgiven you all trespasses."

-    Colossians 2:13 NKJV

"To him all the prophets bear witness that everyone who believes in him receives forgiveness of sins through his name."

-    Acts 10:43 ESV

Do you realize that you have been forgiven? The picture of Biblical forgiveness is so much more than we may even realize. At times forgiveness is glossed over and kind of taken for granted and we can forget just how big of a deal this is.

Imagine with me that you owed someone $100,000. One day that person comes up to you and lets you know they have chosen to forgive your debt with no strings attached. This means you have been relieved from paying that debt altogether. How would this make you feel? For most individuals, it would have taken years, if not a lifetime, to pay off that debt.

Let me try and make this hit closer to where you may currently be at. Imagine the bank comes to you and tells you that all of your school loans, car loans, and the loan you took out for the house were all forgiven immediately. Would you be grateful? What would you do? You would probably be so excited you would be shouting at the top of your lungs.

Here is what I want you to notice. Although it can take many people decades to pay off monetary debts, the reality is that it is payable. However, your debt that God has forgiven is impossible for a human to pay off. You could never have paid for your sins and mistakes; it was impossible.

Pardon is a very similar word to forgive and adds more meaning to what God has done for us. Pardon has the implications of a criminal who has been released from the penalty of the crime they committed. You have been pardoned from your sins. You did the crime but Jesus paid the penalty.

You were in debt but it was paid. You were a criminal but you were released. God graciously let you off, because His Son took your place for the debt that you once owed. This is amazing news! Friends, you are ALREADY forgiven! You are forgiven of every mistake you have made and every mistake that you will ever make. You see, Jesus already paid the price. He didn't just pay for the sins when you didn't know better; He is so merciful that He paid for all the sins you would commit when you knew you shouldn't.

Allow me to take this even one step further. I once heard it preached that "God remembers all of your mistakes, but still chooses to forgive you each time." When I heard that, I immediately had this uneasy feeling about those words. The reason for that is because it contradicts what Hebrews 8:12 says. You see, just because something sounds right doesn't make it right. Do I believe that God is all-knowing? Absolutely, but I also believe He can't lie. What does Hebrews 8:12 tell us? It says "For I will be merciful to their unrighteousness, and their sins and their lawless deeds I will remember no more."

You see, God tells us that He not only forgives, but He forgets. He said that He won't even remember them, meaning He can't even bring it back to His mind because He forgot it. You might say, "Dustin, since God is all-knowing, how can this be?" Well, I don't know. I just know that He has somehow chosen to forget it because He told me He won't remember it anymore.

God not only forgives your sin, but He forgets it too. You don't ever have to wonder if God is keeping a record of your past. He chose to forget and so should you!

You are forgiven!

Declare who God says you are today!

God says my name is Forgiven

I have received complete forgiveness

I am innocent in God's eyes

Thanks to Jesus, I am not guilty

God has forgotten all of my sins and mistakes

Today's Prayer:

Heavenly Father,

Thank You for sending Your Son to pay a price I never could. I am so grateful You have chosen to forgive me for all my mistakes. Not only that, but You said You would remember them no more. I ask You to help me forgive myself and help me to walk in confidence knowing that You see me as innocent. Help me to see myself as You see me.

Amen.

DAY 7 \quad Hello, God says my name is

Healed

"that it might be fulfilled which was spoken by Isaiah the prophet, saying: 'He Himself took our infirmities and bore our sicknesses.'"

- Matthew 8:17 NKJV

"who Himself bore our sins in His own body on the tree, that we, having died to sins, might live for righteousness—by whose stripes you were healed."

- 1 Peter 2:24 NKJV

The price has been paid! Matthew 8:17 states that Jesus "took our infirmities and bore our sicknesses." The word bore used by Matthew is the Greek word bastazó and it means to carry. So, we could read it this way, "Jesus carried our sicknesses."

Let me give you a scenario to understand what this looks like. You and a friend are getting ready to go on a vacation. You have a heavy suitcase sitting by the door and it's ready to go to the car. Since you are taking a little longer than expected, your friend graciously 'carries' your bag to the car. Now, allow me to ask you a question, "Do you have to carry that suitcase to the car?" The answer is NO. Allow me to pose a second question, "Why don't you have to carry the suitcase to the car?" The answer to this question is because someone already

36

carried it out there for you. Someone already did all the hard work for you so that you wouldn't have to.

Just like that suitcase has already been carried, so has your sickness and disease. Sickness, disease, and pain are a result of sin and are part of the penalty for sin. However, Jesus paid the price for your sin and took on all the consequences of sin. Jesus took stripes on His back and in those moments He carried on His shoulders every disease and sickness that would ever come after you.

Often God sees us much differently than we see ourselves. He sees us as clean and we see ourselves as dirty. He sees us as new and we see ourselves as old and used up. He sees us as an heir to all creation and we see ourselves as beggars. Friends, let's line up with how The Creator sees us rather than how we feel or think we look. Remember this, God is much smarter than you, so if He says something about you, it would be good to forget what you think and agree with Him.

God sees you as healed. When you are in Jesus, all God sees is healed. God sees the price already paid and He sees sickness, disease, and pain as defeated. 1 Peter 2:24 says that you WERE healed by the stripes of Jesus. Peter speaks of this as a past event. He is telling you that at the moment those lashes hit the back of Jesus, you were healed in God's eyes.

You need to see yourself as healed today. Don't be moved by what you see or feel. God commands us to live by faith and not by sight (2 Corinthians 5:7), but what does that mean? It means we live by trusting and believing what God said to be true even if it doesn't look like it to our eyes.

Let me challenge the way you may think. We can read 'by the stripes of Jesus we were healed' and view this as a promise to someday be healed in the future. I do believe that can be true, but also believe there is more to it than that. I believe healed is your identity in Christ, meaning you are healed, whether you feel like it or not. For example, my identity was Dustin the moment I was born, not when I understood it. It wasn't a future promise to be Dustin, it's who I was.

Your identity is healed. Healed is who you are now!

Maybe you have been dealing with a physical issue now for years. Maybe you have asked for healing many times and have not seen it. In these moments, sometimes we feel the need to twist God's arm to heal us but God has already expressed His desire to heal us in the payment by Jesus. Rather than asking God to heal you, begin to thank Him for who He has ALREADY made you. Thank God you are healed and speak to the issue. Don't beg God to move the mountain, speak to the mountain.

Your fight isn't against God to get Him to heal you. Your fight is against your enemy who is trying to keep you from who you are. You ARE ALREADY healed! Resist the enemy that is trying to keep you from your identity. Resist the one that is trying to make you carry something that has already been carried. Look at sickness, disease, and pain as an intruder and say, "How dare you try to keep me from who God says I am?"

If you are dealing with physical challenges, don't beat yourself up. There is nothing wrong with you. However, don't let your circumstances change what God says about you. Begin to thank God that you ARE healed. Speak to the mountain in the name of Jesus and stand your ground!

Declare who God says you are today!

God says my name is Healed

I am healthy, whole, and strong

The Spirit of God quickens and makes alive my body

By His stripes, I am healed

I am free from sickness, disease, and pain

Today's Prayer:

Heavenly Father,

Thank You for paying the price for my healing. I can see that Jesus paid the price to make me well. I acknowledge that You see me as healed no matter how I see myself. I know that because of the stripes that Jesus took on His back I can stand before You and say, "By His stripes, I am healed."

Amen

DAY 8 Hello, God says my name is

Valuable

"You were bought with a price [you were actually purchased with the precious blood of Jesus and made His own]. So then, honor and glorify God with your body."

- 1 Corinthians 6:20 AMP

"For you know that it was not with perishable things such as silver or gold that you were redeemed from the empty way of life handed down to you from your ancestors, but with the precious blood of Christ, a lamb without blemish or defect."

- 1 Peter 1:18-19 NIV

If I were to explain the overall theme of this devotional, it would be: don't be consumed by how you feel, what others think about you, who you think you are, or what other people have said about you. Now, of course, if those things all line up with what God says about us, then you should continue to agree with those things. However, we live in a culture that has no concept of self-worth.

We live in a society that is so heavily defined by how we feel and what others think of us. Often, we compare ourselves to others and let that determine our value. Changing our self-image to agree with how God sees us is going to set us free and help us live the life God wants for us. If you believe you are nothing special and feel like you are nothing special, then I'm sorry to say you will probably never amount to anything special in this life, even though you are special. You can limit yourself in this life by how you believe.

God has given humans the ability to choose what they want to believe. God doesn't control us, He lets us choose and our choice can be life or death. Our choice is important. How important? Well, let's ask Jesus. In Matthew 8:13 Jesus said something like this "What you believe is what will be done for you." Basically, Jesus is saying if you believe you are worthless then that is what you will experience. You have the choice to believe what you want.

You are always going to be presented with two choices. God's word or the devil's. The enemy's words are negative. God's words are positive. The devil says you are worthless. God says you are valuable. Here is the thing, the devil knows that what you believe about yourself affects you. Your enemy also knows that God has given you a free will to choose what you believe. That is why he lies to you day and night, hoping you will believe it. Satan knows how valuable you are to God, so he is doing everything he can to convince you that you aren't valuable, hoping you will believe it.

So here we are, God tells us one thing and Satan tells us something else. Satan is a liar and God CAN'T lie. You need to learn to identify what is God and what isn't. It's your job to cast down thoughts, God doesn't do it for you (2 Corinthians 10:5). The Bible tells YOU to resist the devil and he will run away (James 4:7). If you don't know which voice is which, you could be believing a lie and when you believe a lie you end up experiencing it. Believing lies will cause you to live in a place God never wanted you to live.

Here is what I want you to see. I am presenting to you who God says you are. But, you have to choose to believe it. You are worth so much in the eyes of God. Many people "feel" worthless and then conclude that they must be worthless. You need to reject every thought and feeling that opposes this truth. You are so valuable. The Bible tells us in 1 Peter 1:18-19 that you couldn't be bought with silver and gold because it's not worth enough. The only ransom that could pay for you is the very blood of God Himself.

A ransom is a payment that is paid for the release of a prisoner. Jesus paid the ransom for you with His blood. An item is only as valuable as what someone is willing to pay for it. Imagine I take you to a store and there is a bicycle there that you want and it has a price tag of $100. I walk up to the cashier and hand them $100 for that bicycle. Now answer this, how much is the bicycle worth? Well, it's worth $100. What if the price tag said $200 and I paid that $200. Now, how much is it worth? $200. You see, the value is determined by what is paid for it.

Think about what was paid for you! The blood of God's Son.

In God's eyes, you are worth more than all the resources on the planet. Add up all the gold, silver, diamonds, cars, boats, mansions, and everything else and God chose you over those things. Currently, the planet has about $250 trillion in net worth. And you, yes you, are worth more than that to your Creator. God didn't choose to redeem the Earth and its resources, He chose you!

God gave His own Son for you. Jesus gave His life for you. You are so valuable in the eyes of God. You were worth the blood of God.

Declare who God says you are today!

God says my name is Valuable

I am precious in His sight

I was bought with a high price

I am valuable in the eyes of God

God loves me

Today's Prayer:

Heavenly Father,

Thank You for choosing me as the apple of Your eye. You know the number of hairs on my head and You care about every detail of my life. Help me to remember that I am valuable in Your sight even when I don't feel it. I am grateful that You would choose me and I ask You to give me Your eyes for others so I can see them with the same value that You see them.

Amen.

Blessed

"So then those who are of faith are blessed with believing Abraham."

- Galatians 3:9 NKJV

"Blessed be the God and Father of our Lord Jesus Christ, who has blessed us with every spiritual blessing in the heavenly places in Christ."

- Ephesians 1:3 NKJV

Guess what!? You're blessed! Meaning, you are ALREADY blessed. I often hear Christians pray things like "God, would you bless us" or "God, please bless me." There is absolutely nothing wrong with this, I just want to challenge you to think a different way. You don't need God to bless you He HAS ALREADY blessed you.

Look at it this way, if you have called upon the name of Jesus, we know according to scripture that you are a child of God. However, do you go around praying "God, please make me a child of God" or "God, please make me a part of Your family?" If someone does this, it's because they don't realize they ALREADY ARE God's child and ALREADY ARE in His family. They are asking for something that God has already done.

Let's make this even simpler. Imagine I pray something like this: "Father, please make me a human being." Doesn't that sound silly? Well, I already am a human, so why am I asking God for something He already did? God has ALREADY made me a human, therefore there is no reason for me to ask Him to do it. I just acknowledge that it is done and thank Him for it.

Faith in God is complete confidence in what He has said. It means you believe that He is telling you the truth and no matter how you feel or how things look, you acknowledge God's word as truth over reality. So here is the reality: YOU ARE BLESSED. No matter how things look or how things feel, God has already blessed you and sees you as blessed. Look at both Ephesians 1:3 and Galatians 3:9 with me. Galatians 3:9 tells you that you are already blessed if you are a person of faith (in Jesus) and Ephesians 1:3 speaks in the past tense and lets you know that you have already been blessed.

"Well, that's great Dustin. I see that I am already blessed, but what does that mean?" Throughout the Bible, when a person is blessed we see several benefits that follow. A couple of words that are associated with blessed are "happy" and "favored." Blessed has the connotation of a happy person who also enjoys favor with God and with people.

Also, throughout the Bible, especially the Old Testament, when someone was blessed they were granted special favor by God that resulted in joy and prosperity. If you want to see exactly what the blessing of God does check out Deuteronomy 28:1-14. In these verses, we read things like this: everything you touch will prosper and everywhere you go good things will happen. Being blessed also causes all of your business affairs to succeed.

The purpose of the blessing is to draw attention. Deuteronomy 28:10 NLT says "Then all the nations of the world will see that you are a people claimed by the Lord, and they will stand in awe of you." In other words, God's blessing will draw attention to your life and people will see that you belong to Him.

God HAS put His blessing on your life. You are blessed by the creator of Heaven and Earth. This blessing empowers you to be all that God wants you to be and ensures success. God's blessing equips you to be a success everywhere you go.

Being blessed is so much more than we've made it out to be. We say "bless you" when someone sneezes and treat it like just kind words. **The blessing of God in our lives gives us the power to be what God has made us to be.** Blessed is when everything you touch prospers. Blessed is when you and your family love spending time together. Blessed is when your marriage is peaceful. Blessed is when all things work out for your good.

You are already blessed. Everything you touch is blessed (Deuteronomy 15:10). Everything you do prospers.

I want to close with this very powerful word that God says over you. In Deuteronomy 28:8 NLT, God says "The Lord will guarantee a blessing on everything you do."

YOU ARE BLESSED! You are equipped to win!

Declare who God says you are today!

God says my name is Blessed

I am highly favored

God's blessing is on my life

All things work out for my good

God makes me a success wherever I go

Today's Prayer:

Heavenly Father,

Thank You for blessing me. Thank You for equipping me to be who You have called me to be. I am blessed to be a blessing and I am blessed so that I can point to You when good things happen in my life. I am so grateful that You chose me long before I chose You.

Amen.

Royalty

"and (Jesus) has made us kings and priests to His God and Father, to Him be glory and dominion forever and ever. Amen."

- Revelation 1:6 NKJV

"The Spirit Himself bears witness with our spirit that we are children of God, and if children, then heirs—heirs of God and joint heirs with Christ, if indeed we suffer with Him, that we may also be glorified together."

- Romans 8:16-17 NKJV

"For God is the King of all the earth" (and we're His family).

- Psalm 47:7 NKJV

When you have a king or queen that oversees a government on Earth, how do you refer to their family? Well, they are known as the royal family. They are royalty because of their relation to the king or queen who is in charge of the government.

Psalm 47:7 tells us that God is the King of all the earth. And you know what? WE ARE HIS FAMILY! So, what does that make us? Well, it makes us royalty in the Kingdom of Heaven.

The Bible even tells us that we aren't just family, but we are joint-heirs with Christ (Romans 8:17), meaning we inherit everything He inherits as the Son of God.

Hold on! I have even more to tell you. Did you know that Jesus is the King of kings? What kings is that referring to? It is referring to you and me. We have been made kings (and queens). In Revelation 1:6 we are told that Jesus HAS MADE us kings unto God. Look at how important you are! Too many Christians are walking around with their heads down like they are worthless, but you are not worthless. You are royalty in the Kingdom of Heaven. This is not something you earn and it isn't something that happens someday when you are in Heaven; this is who you already are. God sees us as kings and queens on the earth and it's time that we do too.

As of this writing, Queen Elizabeth II is the current queen of England. She knows who she is. It wouldn't matter if one thousand people walked up to her today and said "You're not royalty" and do you know why? It's because she knows who she is. It's because at the end of the day she knows that she is the Queen and what they say about her doesn't change that fact. If someone told her she was worthless she would probably laugh because it doesn't line up with who she knows she is. If you went to Queen Elizabeth II and said "You are not a queen" I am sure she wouldn't go to her room and cry and say "I thought I was important, but I guess I'm not" and "Here all this time I thought I was a queen, but I guess I'm worthless."

When you know who you are you can laugh at the enemy's lies and the lies of the world. The world will tell you that you are worthless. The devil tells you that you can't expect too much because of all you've done in your past. You might hear something like "How dare you to think you are a king or queen, you are nothing." Just laugh at those lies. You are royalty and when you realize who you are these lies won't bother you anymore. Lies can't change the fact that you already are a king or queen, but if you believe them they will keep you from acting like it and experiencing it.

You see, Queen Elizabeth II confidently knows who she is, and it isn't pride or arrogance. Sometimes I think we mistake confidence for pride. If the Queen goes around telling everyone that she is a Queen, does that make her proud? No, she is just sharing a fact, "I am the Queen." It is not any different for you. You must begin to get confident in who you are. It's not pride, it's confidence. When you say "I am part of God's royal family" and "I am a King" or "I am a Queen," you are stating a FACT.

It doesn't matter how you feel, because feelings don't change the truth.

You have been made in the image of God. You have been brought into a family where your Father is the Creator of the universe. He has made you a king. He has made you a queen. You are a son. You are a daughter.

YOU ARE ROYALTY.

Declare who God says you are today!

God says my name is Royalty

I am a King's kid

I am a co-heir with Christ to all God has

I have been made a King/Queen

Today's Prayer:

Heavenly Father,

Thank You for adopting me into Your family. I ask that You would continue to show me what it means to be a child of God. I want to see myself as You see me. You said in Your word that You have made me royalty, so remind me who I am even when I don't feel like it. Help me to discern the lies of the enemy when Satan tries to deceive me. I believe that I am a King/Queen in Your Kingdom.

Amen.

Rich

"For you know the grace of our Lord Jesus Christ, that though He was rich, yet for your sakes He became poor, that you through His poverty might become rich."

-       2 Corinthians 8:9 NKJV

"You will be enriched in every way so that you can be generous on every occasion, and through us your generosity will result in thanksgiving to God."

-       2 Corinthians 9:11 NIV

Over the years, the word rich has developed a bad reputation in the church. All the word rich means is "ABUNDANTLY SUPPLIED." So, if rich is a difficult word for you, just think of abundantly supplied instead.

In speaking of money, I have heard people trying to quote scripture by saying that "Money is the root of all evil." Sadly, this is not what the Bible says. In fact, in 1 Timothy 6:10, we read, "For the love of money is a root of all kinds of evil." Please notice that it is the love of money that is evil, not the money. Money is just a tool in our hands and just because you have money does not mean you love it. We should not assume just because someone has a lot of money that they love it.

Throughout the Old Testament God wanted to give His people abundant provision. For example, men like Abraham, David, Solomon, and Hezekiah all were described as having abundance in provision. God made it a point to give His chosen people more than enough. God's blessing included financial abundance.

So, here's my question: when did this change?

Well, God does not change (Malachi 3:6), so my answer would have to be that it didn't. Many Christians today have the opinion that God will meet your needs and give you just enough, but no more than that. Sadly, so many of God's people think He is a "just-enough" God. If God's character is to only give us what we need, then I have questions for Him.

Why were there leftovers when Jesus fed the 5,000 in Matthew 14:20? And again feeding the 4,000 in Matthew 15:37? God would have known how much was too much, but He gave leftovers. Why did the disciples' nets break and boats sink with too many fish? God knew how many they could hold before giving them too many. In these stories, God was trying to reveal His nature that He is a TOO-MUCH God, a CUP-OVERFLOWER, not just a cup-filler.

"My cup overflows." Psalm 23:5b NIV

In no way am I saying people should be greedy. I also don't want people to crave riches for selfish desires. I am also not saying that you need money to be happy. However, the truth of God's word is that we serve a rich God who has made a covenant with His people to prosper them and give them abundance.

So how does this apply to you?

As Christians, we know there was a great price paid by our loving Savior. Jesus took on the curse of poverty and lack for us. In 2 Corinthians 8:9, the Bible tells us Jesus became poor on our behalf so that we could be made rich. Many times, I have heard it stated that the word rich in this verse is describing spiritual riches. So, did Jesus come to make us spiritually rich? Absolutely, He did, but the word Paul used here for rich is the word "plouteó," which means having many resources or abounding in possessions. Paul is trying to tell us that just like Jesus took our place with sin, sickness, and disease, He also took our place in lack and poverty.

Since the price has already been paid, God no longer sees you as lacking or poor. God sees you "in Christ" so He sees you as abundantly supplied and blessed. You might say, "But Dustin you haven't looked at my bank account, I'm not rich." Look, I am not saying your accounts are currently reflecting this truth, but what I am saying is that God calls things differently than how we see them. God changes our name often before we see the reality of what He says.

Are you going to agree with your circumstances of lack or are you going to agree with God? Just say this, "God, I don't see it right now, but since you say I'm rich, I will just believe it." Maybe you already experience a level of abundance, however, God always has another level for you.

Let me finish with this: When a king and queen have a son he is born a prince. Let's say that the moment he is born, we place him in a pigpen. As he grows up, he stays in the pigpen and it's all he ever knows. He looks in the mirror and just sees himself as dirty and worthless. No one ever tells him who he is, he lives his entire life and dies in that pigpen.

Now, we need to answer some questions. Was he a prince? Yes. Did he look like a prince? No. If you were to ask him if he was a prince, what would he say? No. Does the fact that he didn't know he is a prince make him any less of a prince? No. He couldn't see himself as a prince but it didn't make it any less true. The prince could go his entire life and not know who he is if no one tells him.

Here is the point: He WAS a prince. He was always a prince. He just didn't know it. He didn't feel like it. He couldn't see it.

You may not feel rich. But to God you are. You make not look abundantly supplied. But that is what God sees. In the family of God abundant provision is yours. Your Father is a generous too-much God.

As your friend, I want to issue a challenge to you. You are already rich. It's who you are "in Christ." Don't call yourself poor ever again, that's not your name. God doesn't see you in lack, He sees you as abundantly supplied. Agree with Him, believe it, and say it before you see it. God has business ideas, concepts, wisdom, and strategies for you to walk in this provision. Take some time to ask, be quiet and listen, and then step out on what He tells you to do.

Let me end with a disclaimer. **Wealth without God means nothing**. We are blessed to be a blessing. God gives us abundance so that we can bless our families, others, and support His mission on the Earth.

Declare who God says you are today!

God says my name is Rich

I am abundantly supplied

I always have more than enough and plenty to give

My cup overflows

I am blessed to be a blessing

Today's Prayer:

Heavenly Father,

Thank You for sending Your Son to pay the price for my sins. I am so grateful to be a part of Your family. I believe He took on the curse of poverty for me so I could live in abundance. Just like Abraham was blessed to be a blessing, I believe that You want to bless me to be a blessing. I choose to believe that Your will for me is more than enough so that I have plenty left over to be generous on every occasion. I ask for favor, promotions, business ideas, and wisdom on how to capture and steward my finances in a way that pleases You.

Amen.

DAY 12

New Creation

"Therefore, if anyone is in Christ, he is a new creation; old things have passed away; behold, all things have become new."

-     2 Corinthians 5:17 NKJV

"Then He who sat on the throne said, 'Behold, I make all things new.' And He said to me, 'Write, for these words are true and faithful.'"

-     Revelation 21:5 NKJV

IT'S YOUR BIRTHDAY! Okay, chances are it is not, but play along with me. Imagine it's your birthday, you're getting ready to open your gifts, and friends and family are sitting around watching. You begin to open your gifts with all eyes on you. You open the first package, and what do you see? Socks. Not just any socks, but you can tell these have been worn, not only because of holes and dirt stains, but the smell alone gives it away. As you are opening gifts, you notice something: every one of these gifts is old and used. Along with the socks, you received a few other things, such as used deodorant, an old toothbrush, and dirty underwear. Needless to say, I don't think any of these gifts excited you when you opened them.

On the bright side, you did get something you wanted. You mentioned how you would like shoes for your birthday. And guess what? You got shoes! However, they weren't what you had in mind. They were old, used, and worn out. Can you use your imagination with me? Close your eyes briefly. I want you to imagine being given an old pair of shoes that have been worn through the mud, been to the gym, and have had someone else's feet sweating in them. What do you think they smell like? What do you look like? Do you want them? Are they desirable?

OLD. USED. WORN OUT. NO GOOD. DIRTY. FILTHY. MESSY.

When we think of these words, we often associate them with something worthless. Think back to that pair of shoes. When I describe a pair of shoes as old, used, worn out, no good, dirty, filthy, and messy, what picture do you get in your mind? How much value do you put on those shoes? Are they something you desire or want? When you closed your eyes and tried to picture them you were probably able to see a pair of shoes that are dirty, smelly, and you probably imagined them having a hole or two. Honestly, you may have even scrunched your nose thinking about the smell. Needless to say, these are not something you place any value on.

"Dustin, why are you talking about shoes?" Well, because all of these words (old, used, worn out, no good, dirty, filthy, and messy) are words that Satan will use to describe us. He does his best to make us feel this way. He reminds us of our mistakes and our past, and his goal is to make us look at ourselves the same way we would look at that pair of shoes. When we do that, we feel unwanted and undesirable and feel like we can't be used anymore. You see, Satan wants to diminish your self-worth to the point where you feel worthless. Your reaction to these gifts could be disappointment. And guess what? Satan wants you to look in the mirror and see yourself the same way, with disappointment.

When we believe we are used, old, and dirty, we subconsciously believe we have less value, because that is how we view natural things like those shoes. Satan wants you to see yourself as having no value. Please understand, when I say old, this has nothing to do with age. Old sometimes implies that something is worn out. However, 2 Corinthians 4:16 says that the outward man is perishing, but the inward man is being renewed day by day. The inward man, the real you, is renewed (made new) day by day.

Your enemy desires to make you feel like you don't have value because of everything you've been through. I mean, does anyone have any desire for old deodorant, a used toothbrush, or dirty socks? Probably not, and that's how the devil wants you to view yourself, but you're not worthless, that's a lie. When you believe a lie, you put yourself in bondage to that lie and believe it as the truth.

Would you like to know who you really are? Well, let's have God define you. Not your past. Not your mistakes. And certainly not the devil. In 2 Corinthians 5:17 we read that if anyone is in Christ, they are a new creation. The verse goes on to say old things have passed away and all things have become new. Please notice it does not say old things will someday pass away, and there will come a time when all things will be made new. No, the moment you give your life to Jesus you become a new creation. God does not care what you have done or who you have been. He sees you as a new creation from that moment on, and nothing you do could change that. You are a NEW CREATION!

When I look at words that are associated with new, I think of words like fresh and clean. Don't those sound like great words to be identified with? God sees you as new, fresh, and clean.

Let's go back one last time and pretend it is your birthday. Go back to opening presents. Now imagine this time when you open that shoebox, you see the pair of shoes you have been wanting for months. They are brand-new and have never been worn. They are fresh and clean.

Do you see the difference between these two scenarios? What kind of value do you put on the dirty, used, smelly shoes? What value do you put on the new clean shoes? Satan wants you to see yourself like the smelly and dirty pair of shoes, but I have good news for you: you are a new creation.

God HAS MADE you brand new. Every day that you wake up, in God's eyes you are new, fresh, and clean.

Old things have ALREADY passed away and all things have ALREADY become new. In Jesus, you are new.

Declare who God says you are today!

God says my name is New Creation

I am cleansed

Old things have passed away in my life and all things have become new

I am brand new

I am spotless in God's eyes

Today's prayer:

Heavenly Father,

Thank You for the finished work of the cross. I believe that I am a new creation because I am in Christ. Also, I know that old things have passed away and You have made me new. Thank You for forgiving me, cleansing me, and making me brand new. Even though there are times I may feel filthy, used, and dirty, help me to see myself as You see me which is completely cleansed and pure.

Amen.

Overcomer

"For whatever is born of God overcomes the world. And this is the victory that has overcome the world—our faith. Who is he who overcomes the world, but he who believes that Jesus is the Son of God?"

-     1 John 5:4-5 NKJV

"You are of God, little children, and have overcome them (them is referring to verses 1 and 3 that talks about spirits that aren't from God), because He who is in you is greater than he who is in the world."

-     1 John 4:4 NKJV

Take a moment and picture a champion fighter in your mind. Now, try to imagine what they would look like if they were the biggest, strongest, and quickest fighter on the planet. When it comes to size, they are the largest. When it comes to strength, nobody is stronger. When it comes to speed and quickness, nobody can move faster. Physically, they do not have a single weakness.

If you are having trouble picturing this, let me help you. Imagine someone who towers over everyone else. They stand a foot taller than anyone you know. Their muscles are unlike anything you have ever seen, and they make professional bodybuilders look like middle schoolers.

This fighter wins every fight. In physical abilities alone, this fighter has no one that compares to him. Most of the time, when they are presented with an opponent, they start laughing, because they know nobody is a match for them. This fighter prevails in every fight, subdues every opponent, and always gets the victory. Would this be someone you want to fight? Probably not. Most people would take one look at them and say, "No, thank you."

How this fighter looks to you is what you look like to Satan. You look unbeatable.

Spiritually you are a winner. In the spirit, you look like a champion fighter. In 1 John 5:4-5, we read that anyone that believes Jesus is the Christ is born of God and anyone that is born of God overcomes the world. In other words, if your trust is placed in Jesus then you ARE an overcomer. You are a world overcomer.

In the Bible, we find the word overcome is "nikaó." Nikaó not only means overcome, but also means conquer, prevail, and be victorious.+ God uses this word to describe you. You were designed by God to conquer, prevail, and be victorious.

Let me say this to you: you are a born winner. You were not made to win some and lose some. God created you to win, and in Jesus, you have already been placed in a position of victory. You were made to prevail. You were made to conquer. You were made to get the victory every single time.

+ (Nikao Meaning in Bible - New Testament Greek Lexicon - New American Standard. (n.d.). Retrieved from https://www.biblestudytools.com/lexicons/greek/nas/nikao.html)

You were made to defeat sickness, disease, poverty, lack, stress, worry, strife, anger, addiction, and anything else that would come your way. This is the way God sees you, but guess what? So does Satan.

This puts your enemy in a tough spot. He sees what you look like and he knows there is only one thing he can do about it. So, what does he need to do? He must keep you from finding out who you are. And if he can't do that then he must try to sell you on lies to attempt to trick you. He hopes to keep you from believing that you are who God says you are. If he can keep you from believing that you are already victorious over him, he will keep you battling him and keep you thinking that "Sometimes the devil just wins some battles in our lives." Don't believe this lie, he has already been defeated by our Savior, Jesus.

I'm going to let you in on a secret. Are you ready? You win. No matter what comes your way; you win. How do I know? God said you do. 1 Corinthians 15:57 says "But thanks be to God, who gives us the victory through our Lord Jesus Christ." He didn't design you to win some and lose some. He said you win. You now know the outcome of every challenge you'll ever face: you get the victory. You overcome it.

You are a winner and winner's win. If you ever mess up or feel like you've lost, just get back up and start throwing punches again. I didn't say you would never be in a battle. There will be times it feels like you got punched. But, hang in there!

God sees you as a world-overcoming, victorious winner and it's time you do too.

Remember, you fight FROM victory, not for victory.

Declare who God says you are today!

God says my name is Overcomer

I am victorious

I am born of God and I overcome the world

I am a winner

In Christ, I am more than a conqueror

Today's prayer:

Heavenly Father,

Help me to see myself as an overcomer. I believe in Jesus and You said when my faith is in Him that I would always prevail against Satan and the world. I choose to not give up and choose to see myself as a winner, even in the middle of battles. Thank You for making me a world-overcoming winner.

Amen.

Fearless

"I sought the Lord, and He heard me, and delivered me from all my fears."

\-   Psalm 34:4 NKJV

"For God has not given us a spirit of fear, but of power and of love and of a sound mind."

\-   2 Timothy 1:7 NKJV

Today I am starting with something God shared with me. Often, I enjoy doing quiet time with God while I sit looking over the water, such as a lake, river, or ocean. One particular summer day, I was at a lake sitting and looking out over the water when I noticed a few wasps were flying around. For some people, this may not have been a big deal, but let me tell you how I felt in this situation.

Growing up, I was always extremely afraid of bees, wasps, and any flying insect that could sting. If you knew me well, you had probably seen me run away in terror several times from bees. If I saw a wasp anywhere near me, then I was off to the races and I wasn't ashamed if I screamed. You could have assumed I had been stung several times in my life and that is the reason I reacted this way, but you would be wrong. I have only been stung once in my life and I barely even remember it. I only remember that it happened when I was a child, but I do not remember when, where, or what kind of insect stung me. Honestly, I can't even remember if it hurt or not, even though I assume it did.

So, here is the deal. My whole life, I had lived with this fear. For as long as I could remember, I had this fear. I had always reacted the same way by running as soon as I heard buzzing close by. Running away from bees didn't only take place when I was a child, I also did it as a grown man in my twenties.

Now that you understand that, let's go back to that beautiful summer day when I was sitting out looking over the lake. As I saw those wasps flying around, I was ready to react the same way I had been for twenty-six years of my life. I could feel myself getting ready to get up and run out of there. However, before I could get up, God took the opportunity to show me something. At that moment, God gave me a vision. Please keep in mind, when I say vision it was simply a picture in my imagination. To understand what I mean, it would be like if I told you to picture a vanilla ice cream cone, you could picture it even though you don't really see it, and that is what I saw.

The vision I had was of Jesus and how He would react to the situation I was in. I could see Jesus sitting down as the wasps were flying around Him. All of a sudden, He put His hand out and let a wasp land on His hand, which would have been a nightmare for me at that time. He was completely at peace with no fear, but why should He be afraid? He made them. I then thought about how I usually reacted compared to how Jesus acted, and I distinctly remember God asking me, "Dustin, who are you yielding to when you run away?" He was asking me whose word was I acting on when I ran off and acted on that fear. And whose word was that? Satan. How do I know? Well, because fear doesn't come from God (2 Timothy 1:7).

As Christians, we understand that God moves mightily when we yield to what He tells us. God's language is faith and when people act because of faith, good things happen. Throughout the Bible, we see stories where God tells someone to do something and when people are obedient, God does a miracle. Why does it work this way? It is because God works through humans and He has to work through your free will.

On the other side, we may have been taught less about what happens when we act on what Satan tells us. In the same way that God can bring things to pass when we yield to what He tells us, Satan operates the same way by using fear to get us to act. Satan's language is fear and when we act on fear, something bad happens. When Peter began to yield to fear while walking on the water it caused him to sink. Just like Satan used fear to get Peter's eyes off Jesus, Satan tries to use fear to get your eyes off of God's word.

As I sat at the lake that day, I realized all of these years it was the devil that was telling me to run away in fear and I was listening to him. I was just letting him move me. God would never be afraid of His creation, so as His child, why should I?

After God showed me all of this I was still sitting there by myself with wasps buzzing around. The fear was not gone and I still felt myself wanting to get up and run. But, at that moment I was now faced with a choice. Do I act on the fear I feel or do I hold my ground and not yield? That day I chose to resist fear and did not allow myself to get up.

Make sure you remember what the Bible says about fear. It says in 2 Timothy 1:7 that God hasn't given us a spirit of fear. So, if it isn't from God, where is it from? Our enemy. The Bible also tells us that God delivers us from ALL our fears. God wants to deliver you from every one of your fears.

So, when you begin to feel afraid, you need to ask yourself some questions. Where is this coming from? When you begin to worry or get anxious, ask yourself, who is this coming from? Then remember, God doesn't give you fear, worry, or anxiety. And if it's not from Him we don't want it. If it's not God, we don't want to act on it.

Some people might say "Dustin, I can't help it, I'm just fearful." You are believing a lie. Jesus told people many times "Do not fear" or "Do not let your heart be troubled." Jesus would say the same to you, "Do not let your heart be troubled" (John 14:1). It's our job to guard our hearts. It's our job to fear not. Jesus would never tell us to do something we had no control over.

As for myself, ever since that day at the lake, there have been times I still have to resist that fear when I see a bee flying around. I have to make a choice that I won't move. I refuse to yield to the devil when he puts pressure on me. You see, fear is the devil pressing you to try and make you move. He is attempting to get you to do what he wants.

What do I want you to get from all of this? I want you to see that we all deal with fear. Just because you have a fearful thought doesn't mean you have to let it stay. I always loved the saying "You can't keep a bird from flying over your head, but you can keep it from building a nest in your hair." In the same way, you may not be able to keep the devil from speaking fearful thoughts but you can keep yourself from listening, meditating, believing them, and letting them in your heart.

The one who made you did not make you with a spirit of fear and He has delivered you from ALL fear.

I am not saying that fear will never come. I am not saying you won't "feel" afraid. I am telling you that you don't have to receive it anymore. Resist it. The more you resist, the easier it will get. You can be fearless because that is how God made you. When Satan brings fear to you, reject it, and stand against it. Acknowledge that fear is not who you are, it's just a feeling and you don't have to receive it.

The word of God is the antidote for fear. Fear says "You won't have enough money for your bills", but God says "I'll meet all your needs." It's your choice, which one will you choose when the pressure comes?

All fear is rooted in death. Next time you find yourself 'feeling' afraid be bold enough to tell it "You won't move me." Remember God has delivered you from ALL your fears.

Declare who God says you are today!

God says my name is Fearless

I refuse to fear

I have not been given a spirit of fear

I have been delivered from ALL fears

I resist the devil and he flees

Today's prayer:

Heavenly Father,

Help me to see myself as You do, and that is free from fear. You told me that You didn't give me a spirit of fear. I choose to see myself free from fear. I repent for yielding to fear in my life and will start resisting the spirit of fear when it tries to speak to me. You already see me free from fear, so now I do as well.

Amen.

DAY 15 Hello, God says my name is

Chosen

"You did not choose me, but I chose you and appointed you that you should go and bear fruit and that your fruit should abide, so that whatever you ask the Father in my name, he may give it to you."

- John 15:16 ESV

"Praise be to the God and Father of our Lord Jesus Christ, who has blessed us in the heavenly realms with every spiritual blessing in Christ. For he chose us in him before the creation of the world to be holy and blameless in his sight."

- Ephesians 1:3-4 NIV

If you haven't realized by now, I enjoy using illustrations to help make a point. I believe it helps us understand Bible concepts better when we can imagine a real-life scenario taking place and then linking that with what we are learning about how God sees us. So, guess what? Today, I have... you guessed it... an illustration.

Does anyone remember those days in grade school when you would go outside for recess? How about those days when all the kids would play dodgeball? Now, before all of the students started running around trying to hit each other as hard as they could with a dodgeball, what had to take place? First, you had to pick teams. Everyone had to line up and then two captains started selecting their team. One after another the two captains would take turns picking students. The picks typically started with their best friends and then the captains would start selecting students that they thought would help them win. The picking would typically keep going until there were no more students left. One of the nightmares of many kids was being the 'last pick.'

Every student wants to be picked early and no student wants to be the last picked. Why is that? Well, in those days it defined your value to the captains of the teams. When students are picked early it made them feel valuable. Oftentimes when students were picked at the end it wasn't because the captain WANTED them, it was because they ran out of other options, so they selected them because they HAD TO.

Now think about the last pick with me. How do you think that student would feel? As they wait, every other student is selected before them. By not picking them, both captains have basically said: "We don't want you." Both captains might look at each other and say, "You can have them." After arguing who has to take them, the captain who gets the last pick says, "Fine, come over here," while rolling their eyes. Can you imagine this taking place?

Why am I sharing this with you? If we imagine the Kingdom of God being like those dodgeball teams, many people feel like that last pick. God is the captain and I think some people feel that as God picks His team there are so many other more skilled and qualified people. That can make us feel like God only took us because He had run out of other options to choose from. This could not be further from the truth.

You see, it's often easy for us to look at great men and women of God on TV and say, "Yeah, I can see why God chose them." Maybe there has been a time in your life where you've said, "It's obvious that God chose so and so, but not me." We can look at others and feel like God picked them and He wanted them but He just took us because that was all that was available. Some people may even have the picture in their mind that God is disappointed to have them.

No. God chose you!

I want to let you know something: YOU DID NOT HAVE TO SNEAK ON TO GOD'S TEAM! You did not get on His side without Him energetically waving you over.

Have you ever seen how kids act when their best friend gets picked to be on their team? They are pretty excited. Children are so happy when their best friend is with them. Friend, this is how God looks at you. As you walked towards His side He was emphatically dancing and waving His arms as you approached Him.

Professional sports select players as well. And if you know anything about pro sports you know that many of them do drafts every year to select new players. Do you realize how much thought, time, and energy goes into those picks? They are diligently thought out. No team ever gets to their first choice and says, "Let's give this person a try." They have spent months studying and preparing for who they would like to select.

In the same way that those players are intentionally "chosen" because they are wanted, God chooses you intentionally because you are wanted. He thoughtfully and deliberately chose you. And guess what? God doesn't have any second-round draft picks. You were His number one draft pick.

What I am trying to say is that you were chosen very intentionally. God put thought behind it. He didn't look out at the vast Earth, notice you, and say, "Okay, you can join my team." God sought after you. He thought you were so valuable that He made a deliberate choice to chase after you.

We can see this very plainly in John 15:16, where Jesus said, "You did not choose Me, but I chose you." You were not an afterthought on God's team. God looked out at you and said: "I want that one."

My hope for you today is that you begin to understand just how much value you carry in the eyes of God. Everyone wants to be chosen and nobody wants to be an afterthought. You are not an afterthought. You were chosen.

God chose you. He saw you and said, "I can't live without that one." You are chosen!

Declare who God says you are today!

God says my name is Chosen

I am valuable

I was hand-picked by God

God loves me and He chose me

Today's Prayer:

Heavenly Father,

I am so grateful that You would choose me for Your team. I ask that You would continue to reveal my value to me. Show me my place on Your team, what I was created to do, and what You saw in me when You chose me. I know that I am not an afterthought to You, but I was intentionally picked because You love me. Continue to show me who I am and help me to see the value in others around me. I ask You to help me treat them as You would and that I would reflect Your character to them.

Amen.

DAY 16 Hello, God says my name is

Generous

"You will be enriched in every way so that you can be generous on every occasion, and through us your generosity will result in thanksgiving to God."

-    2 Corinthians 9:11 NIV

"A generous person will prosper; whoever refreshes others will be refreshed."

-    Proverbs 11:25 NIV

While many of the days in this devotional have to do with who God has made you and how God sees you, I believe that today's name comes as a choice of our own. Yes, the reason we may be generous is that we are thankful for what God has done for us, but at the end of the day, we get a CHOICE to be generous or not. As children of God, our Father is the most generous being there is, however, giving is not something He will force you to do. We have been made in His image and we get to be imitators of Him (Ephesians 5:1), but it's our choice to be generous.

Giving does not happen automatically. It comes as a result of a choice. I don't know about you, but I have never had money fly out of my pockets and into the offering just because I wanted to give. I've never heard of anyone buying someone lunch because money jumped out of their wallet and on to the table. You see, giving is a decision. In giving, I get the opportunity to act like God when I choose to be generous. What a privilege!

What am I trying to say with all of this? Well, I am letting you know that today's name, generous, is up to you. You get the opportunity to decide to be generous. There is so much fulfillment in giving. Have you ever given someone a gift and it felt better to give that gift than it would have felt if someone else were to give it to you? I have experienced this often, in fact, around Christmas time I usually do not want to wait until Christmas to give my gifts. Just ask my family. As a child, I would buy something for my parents and ask them to open it right after I bought it. I get so excited to give presents to others that there are times I am often more excited about giving the gift than others are to be receiving it. Jesus was for sure telling the truth in Acts 20:35 when He said, "It's more blessed to give than to receive."

The joy we get when we give is a blessing in itself; however, the Bible does promise more than that to generous people. The Bible lays out some pretty awesome blessings for a person who chooses to be a giver. Let's look at Proverbs 11:25 in the NIV, this verse says that a generous person will prosper. Another translation says the generous will be made rich (NKJV). That verse goes on to say that those who water others will be watered themselves.

Proverbs 22:9 reads similar by saying anyone with a generous eye will be blessed. What does that mean? What do generous eyes look like? This is simply describing a person who is constantly looking for opportunities to be generous to others. This means they are looking through glasses of generosity all the time. When they hear of a need, they think, "Can I help them?" instead of "Well, that's too bad for you guys."

Now, we understand that people should not be able to manipulate us and we don't always need to be the answer, but we should at least be open to any opportunities we see where we could give freely. For example, when my wife and I recently heard someone struggling to buy baby formula, we looked at the situation through generosity glasses, so the next time we were alone we discussed if we wanted to bless them with baby formula. You see, we were listening for an opportunity to be generous, and our eyes were open. They weren't asking us to buy anything for them; we heard the need and immediately thought, "Should we be the solution?" That is what a generous eye is; it's an eye that looks for opportunities to help.

2 Corinthians 9:11 in the NIV says that you "will be enriched in every way so that you can be generous on every occasion." The word "enriched" literally means to be made rich. God does have a desire to enrich you. But why are you being made rich? God does it so you can be generous on every occasion. When you become a person with generous eyes, God wants to give you abundance because He knows you will be willing to give to others.

So, we can see in multiple places in the Bible that God wants people to be generous. However, He also wants to make generous people rich. Why is that? God knows He can trust a giver, so He longs to give them more. He gives them more because He needs vessels to bring His Kingdom into the Earth. He needs generous people that can help propel the vision of God forward in ministries and churches across the globe. Ask any ministry leader or pastor what they are limited by, and you will almost always hear "finances." You are the solution to this problem. God needs to raise Kingdom financiers who can help fund His vision to reach people all over the globe. Do you want to be someone who God can trust with money? Do you want to be a solution to help meet the needs of others? If your answer is yes, then today you need to decide to be generous.

Today I am asking you to say, "God, I choose to be generous." Make a choice that God and others come before yourself.

One practical step that you can take to put this into action is you can set aside money from what you earn to be generous with. This means that when you get paid, you set aside some to give away. In doing this you are making a CHOICE to be generous; you are not waiting to see if anything is left over after you pay for everything else. You are saying, "This is a priority and I am going to do this."

Declare who God says you are today!

God says my name is Generous

I am a giver

I am enriched to be generous on every occasion

I am blessed to be a blessing

God gives me plenty to live and plenty to give

Today's prayer:

Heavenly Father,

I ask for You to help cultivate a generous heart in me. I want to be like You and I want to give as You do. I know that You desire to bless me and that You are looking for people You can trust with finances. Today, I am deciding to be a generous person. I ask now that You would give me eyes to see and ears to hear where You want me to give. As I choose to become a generous Kingdom-minded individual, I ask that You would begin to give me more resources to be a bigger blessing to my family, my church, and those around me.

Amen.

DAY 17

Victorious

"Now thanks be to God who always leads us in triumph (victory and success) in Christ."

- 2 Corinthians 2:14a NKJV (Dustin's added emphasis)

"But thanks be to God, who gives us the victory through our Lord Jesus Christ."

- 1 Corinthians 15:57 NKJV

Have you ever been nervous before? Sometimes people get nervous when they aren't sure what the outcome of something will be. This could happen when you are getting ready to board an airplane for the first time. What does it feel like asking someone out on a date for the first time? Another good one to think about, how do you feel heading into a job interview?

To answer the first question, "Have you ever been nervous before," I'm going to go ahead and answer for you and say "yes." So, what makes us nervous? Well, it's the unknown. It often happens when humans are not one hundred percent sure of a future outcome. It typically happens when we don't know what is going to happen next. Nervousness comes from fear. It is a fear that a situation is going to end up going a different way than you had hoped. For example, you would be nervous getting on a plane because you are thinking something may go wrong and it may crash. Nobody gets nervous that the plane might land safely and ahead of schedule. Again, nervousness, or fear, comes from thinking about a potentially negative outcome.

Let's look at another situation. What happens when a teenage boy approaches the girl he likes to ask her out? First of all, he is probably sweating profusely as he approaches her. But, why would he be nervous? He is nervous because he doesn't know how she will answer and there is a chance that she tells him "no." He is nervous about a negative outcome.

In our last situation, let's talk about the big job interview. How are you feeling the night before? Well, you may find it hard to eat or sleep because you are so nervous. Again, allow me to ask, why are you nervous? It is because you are unsure of the outcome. There is a chance that they don't like you, they tell you no, and you miss out on the job of a lifetime. The nervousness is rooted in the fear of an unwanted outcome.

Let's go back to that person who was nervous and sweating on the plane. If you catch up to them after the flight and ask them, "Are you nervous about the flight you just went on?" What would be their response? Their answer would be "No." Take that same boy who asked a girl out on a first date and fast-forward to their 25th wedding anniversary. If you ask him "Are you nervous to ask your wife out for dinner tonight?" His answer would also be "No." Lastly, think about the person that was up all night worried about their interview. Moments after they get the call that they are hired would they be nervous about the interview? No.

Why are these same individuals no longer nervous about the same situation? It's because they now know the outcome.

You see, nobody gets nervous when they already know what the outcome will be. If we already know what is going to happen, then we have no worry, anxiety, or fear. So, what does this have to do with today's word, victorious? Well, it's because as humans, we can often get nervous when we are in the middle of a battle. When the devil attacks us or a storm comes our way, we can begin to question if we are going to make it out alive.

Even when you are in the middle of a battle, God already sees you as victorious. He already knows your future and sees you as a winner. No matter what comes your way, God has promised that you will win. We know this because 2 Corinthians 2:14 tells us that God ALWAYS causes us to triumph. Well, the word triumph can be defined as "victorious or successful." That means that we can then read 2 Corinthians 2:14 like this: God always causes us to be victorious and successful.

Please take a moment and notice something with me: does 2 Corinthians 2:14 say God sometimes causes us to triumph? Does it say every once in a while God will cause you to triumph? No, it says He will ALWAYS cause you to triumph. The word "always" means on all occasions, forever, and repeatedly. God causes us to have victory on all occasions, forever, and repeatedly. There isn't one occasion where God wants you to lose. God is a winner, and He made you in His image. God promised that, if you would hold fast, He would always give you the victory. In the middle of a storm, it can feel like you are getting beat, and it can even look like you are going to get beat. But guess what? You win.

God has already said His plan is for you is to be victorious all the time. So, who is fighting against you, who is trying to defeat you, who is sending problems, storms, and trouble? It's the devil. Jesus did say that trouble would come, but He never said it would beat you. In the situations you go through, you don't have to be nervous, and do you know why? You are already the victor. The victory is already sure. The devil has been defeated.

Let me go back to that airplane one last time. If that nervous individual KNEW without a doubt that their flight would fly and land safely on time before the flight even took off, how would they act? Even if there was some turbulence they would still rest and be at peace.

When you face turbulence in life, you can rest ALREADY KNOWING the outcome. You win.

Your Heavenly Father is sitting on the other side of everything you could ever go through and He is saying "YOU WIN!" You see, it's not "When I win this battle" or "When I overcome this trial, I will be victorious." You already are victorious. You just might not see it yourself yet. God names you victorious before the battles are over. Choose to see yourself as God sees you. Since you already know you win, how should you act? Sit back and enjoy yourself as you look forward to how God gives you this victory.

What would happen if we chose to believe we already have the victory? What if we begin to see Satan for what he is? A lying defeated foe. You'd never have another worry or fear in your life.

Stand firm knowing that YOU WIN, even before the fight!

Declare who God says you are today!

God says my name is Victorious

I am a winner because God is with me

God always causes me to triumph

Greater is He that is in me than he that is in the world

Even in storms, I stand firm knowing that my victory is sure

Today's Prayer:

Heavenly Father,

Thank You for making me victorious. I know that I have been made a winner in Jesus. I ask for You to continue to show me how You see me. Since I am on Your team I know that I am always on the winning side. In the moments where I am in a battle help me to remember that You have already made me a victor and I will come out on top.

Amen.

DAY 18
Hello, God says my name is

Favored

"For you, O Lord, will bless the righteous; with favor You will surround him as with a shield."

- Psalm 5:12 NKJV

"A good man obtains favor from the Lord."

- Proverbs 12:22 NIV

Take a moment with me and imagine the first person to ever see a fire. As they stare at the beautiful red, orange, and yellow colors their hand creeps towards the flames. Questions are running through their mind. "What is this?" "What does this do?" "Can I hold it?" All of a sudden, their hands get too close to the flame and "OUCH!" At that moment, they learned a lesson. What was the lesson? Don't touch fire because it burns. This person is most likely going to tell their friends and their family exactly what happened. But, why?

You see, they are not going to tell the story for entertainment purposes. They are telling others so that THEY DO NOT DO THE SAME THING! In the same way, the Old Testament stories are not recorded for only historical value (although they provide that); we were supposed to learn from them. We are supposed to read their stories, identify what went wrong and why so that we do not make similar mistakes.

You may be asking yourself, "Dustin, what does this have to do with today's name?" To that, I say, "Hold on, we'll get there." Since this devotional is all about our identity, I think it is valuable to remind ourselves WHY it is so important to know who we are and what can happen if we don't. Just like the fire could burn someone who isn't told, someone who doesn't know how God sees them could face unnecessary problems.

Let's look at the story of Israel when they sent spies into the land of Canaan. At this point, God had already told Israel to "Go in and possess the land" (Deuteronomy 1:8). God would not have told them that if they could not do it. When the spies came back from scouting out the Promised Land, ten of the spies had this to say: "We seemed like grasshoppers in our own eyes, and we looked the same to them" in Numbers 13:33 NIV. The next verse goes on to say that everyone who heard this cried, or in other words, they believed they were grasshoppers as well.

Now, pay attention to this. They came back and said they saw themselves as grasshoppers and watch this, "We looked the same to them." Here is my question for those spies: how do you know what you look like to them? They didn't go into the land and talk to the people of Canaan. Who told them they looked like grasshoppers? You see, they projected what they thought of themselves and assumed everyone saw them like that. God told them, "Take this land, I'll be with you and you are strong enough," but Satan said, "You're too small, you can't do this." Israel had identity issues. They did not see themselves how God saw them and because of that, THEY MISSED OUT ON WHAT GOD HAD FOR THEM. And guess what? It wasn't God's fault.

Here is what you need to take from this story: it is so valuable how you see yourself. Your life can be affected and you can miss out on something God has for you if you don't know who you are.

So, with all of that being said, today I introduce you to your name, "Favored." Here is what you find when you search for the Biblical definition of favor; it means gaining approval, acceptance, or special benefits (blessings).* To be favored means that you not only have God's approval but He is consistently giving you tangible special blessings. Allow me to give you some examples of what favor might look like.

When you get a job you don't deserve or qualify for.
That's favor.

You get a raise or promotion at work.
That's favor.

The car you want goes on sale the week you start looking.
That's favor.

Someone pays for your dinner.
That's favor.

The house you want has a price drop.
That's favor.

The simplest way to describe God's favor on your life is that GOOD THINGS ARE HAPPENING FOR YOU ALL THE TIME. God even takes bad things and turns them into good (Romans 8:28).

*(Favor. (n.d.) In Bible Study Tools. https://www.biblestudytools.com/dictionary/favor/)

Sometimes we look at others and assume, of course, they have God's favor, but we forget it is on our life as well. Many people think they have to earn God's favor and it comes based on how good we are. We may even have the thought that if we please God then maybe He will look favorably at us, help us, and bless us.

However, this is untrue. The Bible says in Psalm 5:12 that God surrounds the righteous (that's you, please see Day 1) with a shield of favor. What does that mean? It means favor is ALREADY SURROUNDING YOUR LIFE. It means every direction you go, favor is out in front of you. It means that everything you put your hands to will have success (Deuteronomy 30:9). It means that no weapon formed against you will prosper (Isaiah 54:17). It means blessings show up everywhere you go (Deuteronomy 28:6).

Please understand the favor of God is on you now. It is surrounding you. The only thing holding you back is... you! Jesus Himself said "It will be to you as you believe" (Matthew 8:13).

Do you believe you are favored?

It may look like nothing has gone your way the last twenty-five years, but don't let that move you. Choose today to believe YOU ARE FAVORED!

Declare who God says you are today!

God says my name is Favored

God's favor surrounds me

Everything I touch succeeds

God makes all things work out for my good

Good things happen to me all the time

Today's Prayer:

Heavenly Father,

Thank You for giving me Your favor. I ask that You would begin to open my eyes to those special blessings You do for me, both big and small. I believe the Word that says there is a shield of favor around me and even when I can't see it, I refuse to believe that it is not there. I am also asking that You would continue to give me favor with those around me and grant me success in the assignment You have called me to accomplish. As I begin to walk in Your favor as I have never experienced before, I ask that Your goodness would be so evident in my life that others want to know You, the "God of favor."

Amen.

Free

"It is for freedom that Christ has set us free. Stand firm, then, and do not let yourselves be burdened again by a yoke of slavery."

- Galatians 5:1 NIV

"So if the Son sets you free, you are truly free."

- John 8:36 NLT

YOU ARE FREE! Free from sin, sickness, disease, poverty, addictions, anger, depression, fear, or any other bondage.

If you do a Google word search for the definition of free, you will find this as one of the definitions: "no longer confined or imprisoned." As I was reading over this I noticed that Google will use the words in a sentence so we can see how the word is used in our language. The sentence for this definition was this: "the researchers set the birds free."

From that sentence, I would like you to take a moment and imagine two birds in a cage. Someone walks outside, sets the cage on a table, and opens it. The person walks away and leaves the birds there. Now, at that moment one of the birds flies out of the cage and lands in a nearby tree. Here is the question I want you to answer: which bird is free? The answer is both. Both birds are free, but only one has taken advantage of this. The bird inside the cage is just as free as the bird that flew out.

One reason the bird might stay in the cage is ignorance. Maybe the bird inside the cage didn't know the door was open. It could stare at the wrong side of the cage, waiting for the cage to open for the rest of its life and would die in captivity, even though it was free. This bird stayed in its cage because of ignorance or lack of knowledge.

The second reason the bird would stay is by choice. The bird could hear the cage open but decide to stay in the comfort of the cage. Or, maybe the bird decides to fly outside for a few minutes but chooses to come back into captivity.

In all of these situations, the bird in the cage was free. The bird either stayed in the cage because of a lack of knowledge or chose to live in bondage. Just because the bird wasn't experiencing freedom didn't mean that it wasn't free.

Believers can be in bondage for the same reasons as that bird. They either don't know they are free or they choose to stay in bondage. The Bible tells us that Jesus HAS ALREADY set us free. Check out Galatians 5:1, where it says, "It is for freedom that Christ has set us free. Stand firm, then, and do not let yourselves be burdened again by a yoke of slavery." Notice it says Christ HAS set us free, not that He is going to. This has already taken place. Don't let the thief lie to you anymore. Maybe you don't feel free? Maybe you don't look free? It doesn't matter, you're free.

Just because you aren't experiencing freedom in an area of your life doesn't mean you aren't free.

Galatians 5:1 first addresses someone who would be ignorant of this truth by saying, "Hey, Christ has already set you free, you don't have to be in bondage." This verse then goes on to address that it can be our choice to live 'burdened' by reminding us, "Do not let yourselves be burdened." Choose to believe you are free and choose to live free.

Jesus has opened the prison doors in your life. The cage doors are open. You are no longer imprisoned by your enemy. God sees you as free! Stop believing the lie that you are not free because of what is going on in your life. Sometimes I hear Believers say "If I could just get free of _____" (you can fill in the blank). No, you are free, but as long as Satan keeps you believing that you aren't yet because of your circumstances he will keep you staring at the wrong side of the cage, thinking it isn't open.

You may not feel free. You may be feeling bound. Are you in a position where you don't feel free but are not sure what to do? Here is where you start: begin to thank God that you are free now.

Faith says, "God I believe You over my feelings, so if You say I am free, then thank You, Lord, I am free."

Declare who God says you are today!

God says my name is Free

The Son has set me free

I am free from sin

I am free from bondages

Jesus opened the prison doors and I am free

Today's Prayer:

Heavenly Father,

Thank You for opening the prison doors in my life. I can see that I am already free. I am now asking You to help me walk out my freedom. If there is any area of my life where I have chosen to stay imprisoned I am asking for You to show me. If I have been ignorant in areas of my life, show me. I choose to walk out the freedom You have paid for. I choose to see myself as free even when it looks like I may be bound. By Your grace, I am free and will always be.

Amen.

DAY 20

Hello, God says my name is

Saved

"For 'whoever calls on the name of the Lord shall be saved.'"

-       Romans 10:13 NKJV

"That if you confess with your mouth the Lord Jesus and believe in your heart that God has raised Him from the dead, you will be saved."

-       Romans 10:9 NKJV

"For God did not send His Son into the world to condemn the world, but that the world through Him might be saved."

-       John 3:17 NKJV

I was saved at the age of ten years old. I still remember my dad kneeling by my bedside to lead me in prayer to invite Jesus into my life. This happened shortly after he had given his own life to Jesus. However, it wasn't until I was twenty when God got a real hold on my heart and I started to live for Him. Even though I had given my life to Jesus, there were times during those ten years when I questioned if I was saved. Since I wasn't living for Jesus in my teenage years, there were many times I questioned, "If I died, would I go to Heaven?"

Here are some other questions I may have asked myself. Am I really saved? Did I lose my salvation?

Maybe you've asked yourself similar questions at some point in your life. I believe there are many Christians that still wrestle with these kinds of questions. We all want to know our eternity is secure, so is it?

Let's examine a few promises from the Bible.

"For God so loved the world that He gave His only begotten Son, that whoever believes in Him should not perish but have everlasting life. For God did not send His Son into the world to condemn the world, but that the world through Him might be saved."
- John 3:16-17

"That if you confess with your mouth the Lord Jesus and believe in your heart that God has raised Him from the dead, you will be saved. For with the heart one believes unto righteousness, and with the mouth confession is made unto salvation."
- Romans 10:9-10

"For 'whoever calls on the name of the Lord shall be saved.'"
- Romans 10:13

Here is the main thing I want you to notice about all of those verses: all of them together say something like this, "If you believe that Jesus died for you and you call upon His name to ask Him to save you, then you **will be** saved."

Here is my question: have you called upon the name of Jesus? If your answer is yes, then guess what, YOU ARE SAVED! Just like in my teenage years, the devil can sometimes get in our heads because he wants us to ask questions like "What if I am not really saved?" Another question the devil wants you to ask yourself is "What if I didn't really mean it when I asked Jesus to come into my life?" Honestly, the fact that you would even ask yourself that question tells me that you meant it. If you didn't want Jesus in your life, you wouldn't be asking this. Satan wants you to question if you are saved so that he can keep you living in FEAR.

And think about this: if you weren't saved, why would the devil even be bringing this up? He is a liar so the fact that he is even talking to you about this should tell you something!

Listen to how confidently Romans 10:13 says you are saved, "Whoever calls on the name of the Lord (to save them) shall be saved." The Bible says this in more than one place. Please notice that it never says, "If you call on the name of Jesus you might be saved," it says you WILL BE. Don't allow Satan to make you question your salvation.

Maybe there have been times you felt like you walked away from the Lord. Maybe there have been seasons in your life when you lived in sin and you knew better. It is in these moments where we can question our salvation.

As humans, we sometimes think people can lose their salvation based on their actions. Good works couldn't earn salvation so why do we think we need them to keep it? Here are some questions to think about: "How many bad works are enough to lose your salvation?" "How much sin is too much sin that you are no longer saved?" Let's say you give Jesus your life, leave the church, and then tell one lie. Are you lost? What if you tell two lies? Two hundred lies? How many lies are too many that you are no longer saved? It is not based on your actions, it is based on grace.

You could not earn your salvation by works and you don't keep your salvation by works.

Now, allow me to say this: I DO NOT condone living in sin. Sin will cause you to live an unfulfilling life that never experiences all the blessings God has for you. Sin causes us to live a life below what God has for us. God can never fully pour out His blessing on us when we live in sin.

But, I do want you to be confident about your relationship with Jesus. Salvation is a free gift you could never earn through your works; therefore, God won't take it away based on your works. There may be times you feel like you've walked away from God but God will never walk away from you. Even when you mess up God is right there with you saying "I love you."

Maybe you feel like you keep missing it. If you have been living in sin, simply confess your sins and then stop letting Satan beat you up by telling you that you are not saved. When you called upon the name of Jesus, you were saved, once and for all. However, Satan is the one who wants you bound in a sinful lifestyle to keep you living in condemnation so you won't live the confident life that God has for you.

God is not mad at you. He loves you. Salvation is a free gift that could never be earned, it can only be received.

When you called upon the name of Jesus YOU WERE SAVED!

You are saved.

Declare who God says you are today!

God says my name is Saved

I am redeemed

I have been purchased by the blood of Jesus

My eternity is secure

Today's Prayer:

Heavenly Father,

Help me to see my eternity is secured. I believe the blood of Jesus paid for me. When I called upon the name of Jesus I believe I was saved as the scriptures say. I ask that You would continue to work in me so that I may see my life change on the outside, just like I have changed on the inside. Father, I ask You to forgive me if I have ever held back from following or pursuing You. I have chosen to make Jesus my Savior and I will live for Him.

Amen.

Masterpiece

"For we are God's masterpiece. He has created us anew in Christ Jesus, so we can do the good things he planned for us long ago."

-       Ephesians 2:10 NLT

"So God created mankind in his own image, in the image of God he created them; male and female he created them."

-       Genesis 1:27 NIV

What would be your guess as to the highest price that has ever been paid for a painting? Without using Google, make a quick estimate. What would be your number? I am unable to make a genuine guess because I already looked it up, but I would assume I probably may have guessed around $10 million. When I asked my wife her guess was $2 million. Needless to say, we were way off!

"Salvator Mundi" was painted by Leonardo da Vinci and is the most expensive piece of artwork ever sold. If you Google the value of this painting you will find out that it sold for $450 million.

What would make someone pay that much for artwork? There are millions of paintings all over the planet. It's not difficult to get artwork. If you go to any kindergarten classroom you can probably pick up a painting for free.

The reason that someone is willing to pay so much for this piece is that it is a MASTERPIECE.

The definition of a masterpiece is "a person's greatest piece of work."^ A masterpiece is often viewed as the pinnacle of an artist's career. These works of art can be extremely valuable for many reasons, such as the quality of the work, the amount of time invested in it, and the tremendous attention to detail. Every brush stroke is diligently thought out and calculated by the artist.

That brings us to your name for today, MASTERPIECE. God calls you His masterpiece, His "greatest piece of work." Ephesians 2:10 says that "we are God's masterpiece. He has created us anew in Christ Jesus, so we can do the good things he planned for us long ago."

I want you to see how amazing, valuable, and beautiful you really are. Take a moment to think of all the work of God's hands. The beautiful oceans. The scenic mountains. The beaches of Hawaii. The gorgeous terrain of New Zealand. The stars and planets in the sky. He made all of these, but you are what He values more than anything. The creator of the Heavens and Earth made you in His image (Genesis 1:27) and considers you His "Greatest work."

Da Vinci created many pieces of art, but very few are masterpieces. God created many things, but only mankind is His masterpiece.

^ (Masterpiece. (n.d.) In Dictionary.com. https://www.dictionary.com/browse/masterpiece?s=t)

The devil wants you to question your value. Your enemy tells you that you don't matter, you were an accident, and you have no beauty. He wants you to think you are worthless. These are lies. However, when we don't know the truth, we will often believe his lies.

You are an amazing creation. You have so much value in God's eyes and you were not an accident. You may not feel like a masterpiece, but we are renewing our minds to see ourselves how God sees us, not how we see ourselves. Choose to believe that God means it when He says "You are My masterpiece." God did not make you on an assembly line. God put intricate detail into you. There is only one like you and you are rare and valuable.

Artists do not create a masterpiece to hide it, hoping that no one sees it. Artists aren't ashamed of their masterpieces; they are often what they want to be known for. God isn't ashamed of you. You were never meant to be hidden. As God's masterpiece, He created you to show you off because you were fearfully and wonderfully made. (Psalm 139:14).

Stop believing any lies that you don't have value or that maybe others have value but you don't. You are one-of-a-kind and God only made one like you. Be happy about how God has made you.

You were made in the image of God. You are God's greatest piece of work. You are a masterpiece.

Declare who God says you are today!

God says my name is Masterpiece

I am valuable

God has made me in His image

I am God's treasure

Today's Prayer:

Heavenly Father,

Thank You for making me into a masterpiece. Help me to see myself as You see me. Expose the lies in my life that I have believed about who I am or how I look. I ask that You would give me wisdom on ways that will bring honor to You with my body. I believe that I was not an accident. I am valuable and I am wonderfully and beautifully made in Your image.

Amen.

DAY 22 Hello, God says my name is

Ambassador

"We are therefore Christ's ambassadors, as though God were making his appeal through us. We implore you on Christ's behalf: Be reconciled to God."

- 2 Corinthians 5:20 NIV

"For our citizenship is in heaven."

- Philippians 3:20a NKJV

I am sure you have heard the term ambassador many times. You may have even heard it before in the context of 2 Corinthians 5:20. However, today I hope to give you further insight into your identity as an ambassador of Heaven. First, before we get started, what exactly is an ambassador? One of the definitions of an ambassador is an "authorized messenger or representative."#

Think of this in the context of you being an ambassador for Christ sent from Heaven's government into the world. As an ambassador for Heaven, you are an authorized messenger sent to represent your government. God has sent you, as His representative, to enforce His government in the Earth.

(Ambassador. (n.d.) In Dictionary.com. https://www.dictionary.com/browse/ambassador

You are God's ambassador.

You were never created to beg God to do things. You were created to find out what God wants through His Word and then go out and enforce it. Sometimes when you touch on these things people think that we are telling God what to do. This is absolutely not true. We are pressing into God, finding out what He wants (through the study of His Word and prayer), and then being His vessel by going out to release Heaven into the Earth. We will touch on this in a little bit later when we see how Jesus operated.

Here is one thing you need to understand before we move forward today: an ambassador is not a citizen of the nation they reside in, but rather they are a citizen of the nation that sends them. You see, this is what Jesus meant when He said: "I am not of this world" in John 17:16. Jesus was sent by God, Heaven's government, to accomplish a mission. Jesus was always a citizen of Heaven, but He was sent into the Earth to enforce God's will. And now, the same way that God sent Him, Jesus sends you (John 20:21).

If you are a citizen of the United States and I asked you to show me your passport, it would say the United States of America on it. If you had a spiritual passport that we could see, it would say a citizen of Heaven. This is because the Bible tells you that your citizenship is in Heaven (Philippians 3:20). There will come a day when you actually reside there, but for now, you are on a temporary mission to represent your government, the Kingdom of Heaven, in the Earth realm.

Please remember that Jesus was the original ambassador from Heaven. As an ambassador, sent to represent Heaven, Jesus would enforce God's will on the Earth. When reading the

Bible, I never see Jesus begging God to do things. Whenever Jesus went to heal someone or cast a demon out, you don't hear Him say "Hold on, I need to check and ask my Father if He will let me do this." And why didn't He? It's because Jesus knew the will of God (from His quiet times with the Father) and then did what God told Him to do. Jesus released Heaven, He didn't beg Heaven to intervene. Jesus was our model and example to imitate (1 Corinthians 11:1) and we were called to operate as He did.

So, let's further study how Jesus, as our example, operated as an ambassador sent by the Father. Do you remember when Jesus said "I only say what I hear my Father say" in John 12:49? The Father would tell Jesus what to say or do, Jesus would say it or do it, and then the Father would do the work (John 14:10). In other words, Jesus would find out what God's will was, Jesus would enforce it, and the Father would back Him up.

Take a moment and really listen to what Jesus was saying in John 5:30 NLT. "I can do nothing on my own... I carry out the will of the one who sent me, not my own will." First of all, Jesus Himself said "I can do nothing on my own," which sounds similar to the position we are in. However, He goes on to say "I carry out (ENFORCE) the will of the one who sent me." Then in John 14:10, we read where Jesus said He doesn't speak His own words. Jesus came to be God's voice in the Earth.

Think about this: many people think God is completely in control of everything, including the weather. If that is so, then Jesus rebuked His Father when He spoke to the storm. You see, God was not in control of that storm, but Jesus (as an ambassador) enforced God's will and told that storm to "Be still." This is how you were created to operate, my friend! God has put an amazing amount of responsibility in your hands. It is quite humbling when we realize just how much God has entrusted us with. He is counting on you to find out what His will is and then go into the world and enforce it and push back the kingdom of darkness.

As an ambassador, you have been sent by the King of kings to enforce His government here. This is why the scriptures say things like "whatever you bind... will be bound in Heaven" (Matthew 18:18) and "if you say to the mountain be removed... it will be removed" (Mark 11:23). God has authorized you to act on His behalf and He works through His representatives in the Earth that are here enforcing His government.

You are not of this world (John 15:19). You are a citizen of Heaven here on assignment as long as you have breath in your lungs. You do not need to beg God to move. Your job is to spend time in prayer and in His Word to find out what He wants to be done on the Earth and then go out and release Heaven.

Too many Christians are begging God to move the mountains in their life and not realizing that God has told them to speak to them. You were called to imitate Jesus. Jesus spent quiet time with the Father and then enforced His Father's will.

You are God's mouthpiece. You are an ambassador sent to represent Heaven. You are Heaven's ambassador called to reveal God's goodness.

Declare who God says you are today!

God says my name is Ambassador

I am a citizen of Heaven

God has sent me to represent the Kingdom of Heaven

I speak to the mountain and it moves

Today's Prayer:

Heavenly Father,

Reveal to me on a deeper level the revelation of being Your ambassador and representative for Heaven on the Earth. I believe I am called to represent You by showing people how You look and act. I am also called to enforce Your will and government the same way Jesus did. I am asking You to give me a greater understanding of Your will. Show me areas of my life where I have lived below my rights as a citizen of Heaven. I am so grateful that You would choose me and it's an honor to represent You and carry Your word into the Earth.

Amen.

DAY 23   Hello, God says my name is

Bold

"The wicked flee though no one pursues, but the righteous are as bold as a lion."

- Proverbs 28:1 NIV

"So that we may boldly say, The Lord is my helper, and I will not fear what man shall do unto me."

- Hebrews 13:6 KJV

Lions are very bold. There is a reason they are called the king of the jungle. Lions may not be the biggest, fastest, or strongest animals, but they sure act like they are! Lions aren't scared of anything. They go into any battle BOLDLY with no fear and have the mindset that they will win every fight. AND GUESS WHAT? God compares you to those lions. God says you have that same boldness inside of you. How do I know that? Easy. The Bible says that the righteous are as bold as a lion and since you are righteous (see Day 1), that means God was talking about you.

YOU ARE AS BOLD AS A LION. God doesn't need to give you boldness, you ALREADY have it.

"But, Dustin I don't feel bold" you might say. Please remember this devotional is dedicated to helping you see yourself as

God sees you. There is often a difference between how we see ourselves and how God sees us. We are on day twenty-three so hopefully, you have already realized this by now!

It's possible that you currently see yourself without courage and see yourself as timid, but none of that matters to God. God sees you as bold. We often see ourselves as less than God sees us and that causes us to live at a lower level than God wants. We have an identity issue any time that we see ourselves differently than how God sees us.

In the book of Judges, there was a man named Gideon who had an identity issue. When we first find Gideon, he was attempting to hide wheat from an enemy army because he was afraid of them. God came to Gideon (while he was hiding his wheat) in Judges 6:12 and said: "The LORD is with you, mighty warrior." A few verses later Gideon responds to God by saying "My clan is the weakest in Manasseh, and I am the least in my family" (Judges 6:15). In other words, Gideon responded to God by saying, "You have the wrong guy, I am not a mighty warrior, I am the least important person in the most insignificant family around." When Gideon looked in the mirror, he didn't see the same thing that God saw. Gideon saw himself as small, weak, unimportant, and insignificant. God saw a mighty warrior.

Sometimes when we look in the mirror we see something different than what God sees. Any time that you deny what God says about you, YOU ARE CALLING GOD A LIAR. If God says you are bold and you say "No, I'm not," you just told God that He is a liar. You see, God CAN'T lie. So, when He calls you bold, guess what? You are bold whether or not you see it or feel it.

Gideon's story is often no different than ours. We think we are small and insignificant, but God says we are mighty. Far too often Christians shrink back and let fear dictate their actions because they don't think they are bold enough. They hear stories of others stepping out boldly, wishing they could too, but they stay out of the action while saying things like, "I'm just not that bold."

Would you like to know the opposite of bold? It's timid. And God has not given us a spirit that makes us timid (2 Timothy 1:7 NIV). God has not made you timid. Satan says you are small. God says you are mighty. Satan says you are timid. God says you are BOLD.

What has fear kept you back from doing in your life? Has it kept you from stepping into your destiny? Has it kept you from sharing your faith?

Don't let fear dominate you anymore. You are bold! You are unafraid!

If God be for you who can be against you and the Greater One is on the inside of you (Romans 8:31 & 1 John 4:4).

Step out BOLDLY on the water and watch God do a miracle.

Declare who God says you are today!

God says my name is Bold

I am courageous

Greater is He that is on the inside of me

I am fearless and unafraid

God is for me so who could be against me

Today's Prayer:

Heavenly Father,

Thank You for loving me. Forgive me if I have listened to the enemy's lies about my identity. I'm asking You to help me see myself as You see me. Today I now see that You want me to walk in boldness and confidence. I choose to believe Your word and I believe that I am as bold as a lion. And today I declare that "The Lord is my helper, and I will not fear what man shall do unto me" (Hebrews 13:6).

Amen.

DAY 24   Hello, God says my name is

Strong

"I can do all things through Christ who strengthens me."

-      Philippians 4:13 NKJV

"Let the weak say, 'I am strong.'"

-      Joel 3:10b NKJV

Today, you may be walking through some things that are challenging to you. Life could be difficult right now or life could seem to be going along rather easily. No matter what season you are in, your identity will never change.

Your mouth is always a good barometer of what you are believing. Jesus said out of the abundance of your heart your mouth would speak (Luke 6:45). Basically, what He was saying is that what you believe will eventually come out of your mouth. We need to make sure that what we say is lining up with what God says.

I hear way too often Christians say things like "I'm just so weak." Have you ever noticed how much people always talk about how tired they are? Too often we find ourselves talking about how weak and tired we are. This is usually because it's how we feel so that's what we talk about.

God doesn't tell us to talk about how we feel. In fact, the Bible says a fool vents how he feels (Proverbs 29:11). God tells us to talk about how He sees us. Talk faith, not feelings. What is talking faith? It is simply saying what God says.

One of the best examples of this in the Bible is found in Joel 3:10 where we read "Let the weak say, 'I am strong.'" Again, when most people feel weak, they talk about how weak they are. God specifically says here that when you are feeling weak say "I am strong."

In your eyes you see weak but God sees strong. He sees you differently than you see yourself. God says "say what I see." When you feel your weakest is when you need to say "I am strong" the most.

Gideon went through exactly what we are talking about. Remember what God said to Gideon? At one of the moments he felt the weakest, God came to him and called Gideon a mighty (strong) warrior in Judges 6:12. You see Gideon didn't see himself as strong, but God did. God saw his identity all along and had to tell Gideon who he was because Gideon couldn't see it.

Even at your weakest, God still sees strong. It's hard to say you are strong when you are feeling weak. IT TAKES FAITH TO SAY IT WHEN YOU DON'T FEEL IT.

Philippians 4:13 says "I can do all things through Christ who strengthens me." I want you to notice that it says "I can." It doesn't say I might be able to or sometimes I can. Even though you look weak the reason God doesn't see you as weak is because the Greater One is always with you. God sees you equipped with Christ at all times. How can you be weak when you have the very power of God living on the inside of you?

You are strong.

When God looks at you, strong is what He sees. This is why He tells you that when you feel weak you need to say "I am strong."

God is with you. You are strong in the Lord and the power of His might (Ephesians 6:10).

Declare who God says you are today!

God says my name is Strong

I can do all things through Christ who strengthens me

I may feel weak, but I am strong

I am strong in the Lord and the power of His might

Today's Prayer:

Heavenly Father,

As of today, I choose Your word over my feelings. You are my strength. You are the reason that I can stand up and say "I am strong" even when I feel like I cannot keep going. I ask for You to daily give me the strength to stand against all the schemes of the enemy. You are my God and You are on the inside of me so therefore I am strong enough to handle anything that comes my way.

Amen.

Successful

"He stores up success for the upright; He is a shield for those who live with integrity."

-       Proverbs 2:7 CSB

"The LORD was <u>with</u> Joseph, so he <u>succeeded</u> in everything he did as he served in the home of his Egyptian master."

-       Genesis 39:2 NLT

"Be strong and courageous. Do not be afraid or terrified because of them, for the Lord your God goes <u>with</u> you; he will never leave you nor forsake you."

-       Deuteronomy 31:6 NIV

I believe success can be something that Christians have tried to stay away from. The reason, I believe, is that success is often associated with pride. There is almost a negative connotation that if you want to be successful it's wrong and you shouldn't want that. It also sometimes feels like, if you want to be successful, some people in Christian circles kind of look at you like, "Who do you think you are?"

Today I hope to help you further understand this topic. I want to help you understand why, as Christians, we should want to be successful. First of all, success is a Biblical word. God is not a God of failure, He is a God of success. Other words for success are achieve, accomplish, win, and triumph. Does God ever make a mistake? Does He ever lose? Absolutely not, so He SUCCEEDS in everything He does. If God is a successful God and we belong to Him, we should be successful people.

Let's quickly examine the purpose of success and why you should desire to be successful. The purpose of success is to draw attention to God. In Deuteronomy 28:1-14 God lists out blessings, good things, and successes that He wants to send your way. However, in these verses, there is something hidden in verse 10 that tells us why God does this. Check this out, it says, "Then all the nations of the world will see that you are a people claimed by the LORD, and they will stand in awe of you" (Deuteronomy 28:10 NLT). The purpose of God granting you success is so that everyone else will see that you belong to God. God wants to use your success to draw attention to Himself and His goodness.

A great example of success is Joseph. Wherever Joseph went He found success. He went to Potiphar's house and succeeded. He was sent to prison and succeeded. Finally, Joseph got to Pharaoh's palace and he succeeded. Why was Joseph successful? Well, we find that answer in Genesis 39:2a where we read, "The LORD was with Joseph, so he succeeded in everything he did." Joseph's success was directly correlated to the fact that God was with him. And guess what? Others noticed it too. In Genesis 39:3 we find that Joseph's master could see that God was with him and in Genesis 41:38 Pharaoh noticed that God was with Joseph. The success of Joseph drew attention to God.

In the same way that God used Joseph, God wants to use you today. God wants to reveal His goodness through you as the light of the world (Matthew 5:14) to draw others to Him. God wants you to be a light in the world that will point to Him as your source. Success draws attention to you so you can point people to your God. Essentially, success draws attention to the God you serve.

There is nothing wrong with desiring success, my only question is: whose kingdom are you trying to build? Your own? Or God's?

Now that you see that God wants to use your success, maybe you are wondering what this has to do with you. You might be saying, "that's great and all, but I'm not very successful." I'm not here to talk about your current situation, what you see, how you look to yourself, or even how you look to others for that matter. My purpose is to help you see yourself how God sees you.

God already sees you as successful. You have all the tools to be a success. Do you know why? It's because He is with you. Take a moment and remember why Joseph succeeded. It was because God was with him. Well, guess what, God is with you and He will never leave you or forsake you (Deuteronomy 31:6, Hebrews 13:5). So, let's read Genesis 39:2 with your name in it.

"The LORD is with _____ (your name), so I succeed in everything I do."

Whether you have seen some success in your life or not, God is with you. You have everything you need to be successful. You need to see yourself how God sees you! Just because you have failed does not make you a failure. God is with you! You are a success! Go out and take territory for God. Maybe you have seen some success in your life, that's great, but as long as you have breath in your lungs God wants you to continue to reach further to expand your influence for His kingdom.

Maybe you have never felt like you've been given permission to dream. Take some time today and let yourself dream about getting to the top of your field of work so that you can point as many people as possible to your good Father. Success will give you a larger platform to proclaim the works of God in your life. Success is not bad, it's a good thing, and more importantly, it's a GOD thing.

Declare who God says you are today!

God says my name is Successful

God blesses all the work of my hands

The Lord is increasing me more and more

The Lord is with me so I succeed in all I do

Today's Prayer:

Father,

Thank You for Your word that says You will never leave me nor forsake me. I stand firm on Your promise that You are with me and since You are with me I know that You cause me to succeed in all that I do. You are a God of success and I was made in Your image. I ask that You would better help me understand Your plan for my life. Show me what mountain tops of influence You are calling me to so that I can be a city on a hill that reflects Your goodness. I ask You to use me to draw people to You and Your goodness.

Amen

DAY 26   Hello, God says my name is

Healthy

"He sent out his word and healed them, and delivered them from their destruction."

-    Psalm 107:20 ESV

"So you shall serve the LORD your God, and He will bless your bread and your water. And I will take sickness away from the midst of you."

-    Exodus 23:25 NKJV

You may have the question, "Why we are doing a day for the word 'healthy' when we already did 'healed'?" Across the planet, there are always people under physical attack. Sickness and disease are constantly trying to overtake people, and many times, sickness, disease, and pain can speak loudly in our lives. It is in those moments that we need God's voice to speak louder over us than sickness, disease, and pain.

As you read this today, you are in one of two categories: the first category would be that you are currently dealing with some kind of physical symptoms in your body. The second category is that you feel great, which is awesome, and now is a great time to build your house on the rock of God's word before an attack tries to come.

As humans, we need constant reminders of how God sees us. Why do you think God says things like in Joshua 1:8 that we are to meditate on His Word day and night? God knows that we will believe what we CONSTANTLY feed on. There were even times that Jesus said "again I say" because He had to say it more than once.

Do you remember when you were young and you were taught 2+2=4? After hearing this once, did your teacher say "Now you know it, we can move onto something else?" Absolutely not. You had to be taught 2+2=4 over and over again. You had to hear it repeatedly until you knew that you knew it. Hearing it once didn't cut it.

In the same way, you need a constant reminder that Jesus bore your sicknesses and carried your diseases (Isaiah 53:4). You need to be reminded that by His stripes you WERE healed (1 Peter 2:24). There are so many voices in the world talking about sickness and disease. Fear is running rampant with cancer nearly everywhere you look. Every time you turn on the television you are hearing about new diseases and you are (most likely) being bombarded with thoughts of something being wrong in your body.

There is a war for your life, my friend. Satan does not want you to walk in the health that God has for you. How do I know that God already sees you as healthy? It is because you are in the body of Christ (1 Corinthians 12:27). We need to quit playing with the lie that God sometimes wants people to be sick. Do you want your kids to be sick? Do you think your children need the flu to learn how to obey you or to learn patience? God has better ways of teaching us than sickness and that is through His Word and THE TEACHER, the Holy Spirit (John 14:26).

"But, Dustin, how can God can see me as healthy when I don't look like it to myself?" God does not see you as you see yourself. Our loving Father sees us through the lens of Jesus' blood and the finished work of the cross. He sees you as a member of Christ's body. God was the one that said, "As He (Jesus) is, so are we in this world" in 1 John 4:17. Jesus is healthy and as He is (healthy), so are we in this world. God saw all of YOUR sickness, disease, and pain put on Jesus. Jesus took YOUR sickness, disease, and pain. Jesus took YOURS, so why should you have it?

Sickness, disease, and pain are weapons forged by our enemy and we should resist them with everything we have. Stand against them. Do not yield to them. Do not give in to them and say, "This is just God's will for my life." Satan is a thief that comes to STEAL, kill, and destroy (John 10:10). Sickness is a thief of time, money, peace, family, and so much more. It steals your time when you have to be at the hospital. It steals your money on hospital bills. It steals parents from their children. God hates sickness because of what it does to the creation He loves and that is why it isn't in Heaven.

In closing, remember Proverbs 12:18b ESV which says, "The tongue of the wise brings health." The tongue, or the words, of a wise person, brings health.

A wise person is someone who agrees with God and says what He says even when it doesn't look that way. Be wise, and agree with God, say, "By His stripes, I am healed and I am healthy... He is the Lord who heals me and keeps me healthy" (1 Peter 2:24, Exodus 15:26).

Declare who God says you are today!

God says my name is Healthy

Jesus paid for my sickness, disease, and pain

I am healthy by the stripes of Jesus

I am healed in the body of Christ

As He is, so am I in this world

Today's Prayer:

Heavenly Father,

You are so good to me. I ask today, with a sincere heart, that You would help me to see myself as You see me concerning health and wholeness. Thank You for sending Your Son to pay for sins and everything that resulted from my sins, including sickness. I believe that since Jesus paid the price for me to receive healing in my body. I receive the health that You have for me so that I can run my race and finish my course. You have things for me to do in this life and sickness, disease, and pain are weapons forged against me to slow me down. Help me to walk in health. Show me any areas in my life where I have been deceived.

Amen

DAY 27   Hello, God says my name is

Wise

"If any of you lacks wisdom, you should ask God, who gives generously to all without finding fault, and it will be given to you."

\-   James 1:5 NIV

"In whom (Christ) are hidden all the treasures of wisdom and knowledge."

\-   Colossians 2:3 NIV

WISDOM HAS BENEFITS. Throughout the book of Proverbs, we see numerous benefits to wisdom. Just to name a few, the wise inherit honor (Proverbs 3:5), being wise saves lives (Proverbs 11:30), and healing comes from the tongue of a wise person (Proverbs 12:18). We also see that wisdom brings long life, riches, and honor (Proverbs 3:16). When Solomon asked God for wisdom, God gave him not only wisdom, but also gave him riches, wealth, and honor, or in other words, INFLUENCE. God wants you to have influence. When we are wise and have answers to problems, not only does it help us, but others will seek us out and we can then point to our Creator. Wisdom also has the ability to help you end up in the right place at the right time… every time.

There are times we don't know which way to go in life or we don't know what choice to make. Wisdom from God can answer anything. Which job should you take? Wisdom will help. Who should you marry? Wisdom will help. Which brand of washing machine do we buy? Wisdom will help. Do we buy this house or that house? Wisdom will help. Where do we send our kids to school? (Any idea what I'm going to say next?) Wisdom will help. The point is, wisdom from God can answer anything you need.

With all of that being said, you are wise! You may not feel wise, but God calls you wise. Do you know why? It's because God sees all that He has made available to you. He sees you with the Holy Spirit in you as your teacher. He sees you with the mind of Christ. He sees all that is available to you.

Being wise has very little to do with you but has everything to do with what you have access to at all times. You are wise! Believe it. It's not about you, it's about what God has done in you and for you.

Let me explain briefly why you can AND SHOULD boldly declare that you are a wise person: first, you have the mind of Christ. We find this in 1 Corinthians 2:16 which is telling you that you have access to all that Christ knows, which is EVERYTHING by the way. Second, Jesus gave you the Holy Spirit to teach you. In John 14:26 Jesus said the Holy Spirit would teach you ALL THINGS. All things. That means He will give you the right answer every single time. And where did Jesus say the Holy Spirit would be? He said this great Teacher will be IN YOU (John 14:17). Thirdly, and lastly, Colossians 2:3 says that all treasures of wisdom are hidden in Christ. Well, since you are hidden in Christ and all wisdom is in Christ, you have access to all treasures of wisdom.

Here is what you need to grasp today: God has made you wise. You are wise already. Not because of you, but because of what Jesus has done for you and in you. You have the mind of Christ. You have the Holy Spirit, the Great Teacher, on the inside of you and access to answers.

Wisdom will help you make decisions. Do not allow yourself to go around worried about making the wrong decisions. Making the right decisions is easy. Simply acknowledge God, acknowledge He has the answers, and then just give Him time to answer. He wants to help you more than you want to be helped, just be patient, and give Him time to answer.

Let me end by telling on myself quick. When I was younger and didn't know what God wanted me to do with my life I used to say "I don't know" all the time. It would kind of just slip in after every sentence. It was almost like a filler word for me. Well, this was when God was teaching me that the tongue is like a steering wheel to life (James 5). The more I said I don't know and the more I talked about how I don't know what to do, the foggier things got.

God showed me I needed to change what I was saying. I started saying I have the mind of Christ and I know everything I need to know (1 Corinthians 2:16). 1 John 2:20 says that we "Have an anointing from the Holy One and we know all things." He wasn't saying you will know everything, He was saying that you will know everything that you need to know! It's worked for me and it will work for you too!

You have the mind of Christ! You are His sheep and you know His voice (John 10:27). You are wise!

Declare who God says you are today!

God says my name is Wise

I have the mind of Christ

In Christ, I have treasures of wisdom

The Holy Spirit teaches me everything I need to know

I am His sheep and I know His voice

Today's Prayer:

Heavenly Father,

In the moments where I do not have answers, I choose to look to You. You are my wisdom and I am so grateful that I can come to You boldly anytime I need help. I ask You to help me by giving me wisdom for my daily decisions. I ask for guidance to lead me to the right place at the right time. Thank You for ordering my steps.

Amen.

Well-Supplied

"And God will generously provide all you need. Then you will always have everything you need and plenty left over to share with others."

\-   2 Corinthians 9:8 NLT

"You shall remember the Lord your God, for it is he who gives you power to get wealth, that he may confirm his covenant that he swore to your fathers, as it is this day."

\-   Deuteronomy 8:18 ESV

The first thing I want to mention today is that the term 'well-supplied' is a big word. Although our major topic today will be about your identity with God's financial provision, I wanted to first make a disclaimer before we get started: I know without a doubt that there are some things that money absolutely cannot buy in this life. A good relationship with your spouse, kids, and family cannot be bought. Good health cannot be bought. A great relationship with our Heavenly Father cannot be purchased. Money does not guarantee happiness. However, it is impossible to live a life of peace without financial provision. God never intended you to live a life of financial stress by living paycheck to paycheck and drowning in debts.

I meet many Christians with good intentions, but it's almost as if they are scared of having money. I have heard Christians say things like, "I only need enough for me and my family." Friend, that is the wrong mindset. You need to be believing God for more than enough so you can help others. God's will for you financially is that you not only have all of your needs met, but have plenty left over to share with others (2 Corinthians 9:8).

Many people think money is evil. An often misquoted scripture is "Money is the root of all evil," but I have to let you know this is not in the Bible. Instead, we read that "The love of money is the root of all kinds of evil" (1 Timothy 6:10). Loving money is evil, not having it. Money only magnifies what is in your heart.

Allow me to give you a quick illustration to help you understand what I mean by that.

Is a baseball bat good or evil? Take a moment and answer that question. Well, honestly, the answer is neither. A baseball bat could be used to hit the game-winning home run for your favorite team in the World Series. However, that same bat could be used as a murder weapon. So, again, is the bat good or evil? Neither. A bat is just a tool in our hands. In the same way, money is just a tool. The money will only magnify what is in a person's heart.

God doesn't care if you have money; He just doesn't want money to have you. Ask yourself the question, does God want money in the hands of people that love Him or do evil? On Earth, money is power. Satan is the one that doesn't want Christians to have money, so he hides behind religion and says that money is evil and that it's greedy to have it because he wants it. I am here to expose him.

Christian, you should have money! You should believe God for money to get financially free so you can bless others and fund ministries and churches.

Take a moment to think about the following questions.

What could you do if you had a billion dollars? What could you do for your family? What could you do for God's agenda on Earth?

What if Christians had enough money to buy out every TV station? We could preach the gospel on every channel 24/7.

What if people with God's heart had the money Hollywood has? Imagine the influence we could have!

God wants you to have influence. That's what it's about. Money can bring influence. You can buy TV time to talk about Jesus. You can buy billboards. You can bless people. You can point more people to God. You can get people's attention so that you can point to God. After all, He gave it to you.

Being well-supplied is part of the covenant with God. Read Deuteronomy 8:18, which says, "You shall remember the Lord your God, for it is he who gives you power to get wealth, that he may confirm his covenant that he swore to your fathers." Did you read that? God will give you the power to get wealth to confirm His covenant. Attaining wealth is part of His covenant! "But, Dustin, isn't that the Old Testament?"

Yes, but the promises made to Abraham and his seed are available to us as well in the New Covenant. Read Galatians 3:29. This scripture says that if you belong to Christ, then you are Abraham's seed and heirs to the promises made to him. Every promise in Christ is yes and amen (2 Corinthians 1:20).

So, let me end today by saying this: I am passionate about money because I am passionate about funding God's Kingdom and His purposed in the Earth. You may not look well-supplied in your eyes, but in God's eyes, you already have all the tools to walk in abundance. He sees you with the Holy Spirit on the inside of you to give you ideas, concepts, and strategies. He sees you with the mind of Christ. He sees you with the covenant promise of wealth. You have all the tools to acquire wealth.

Remember this, God called Abraham "the father of many nations" before He had any children and He will call you well-supplied before you look like it.

At the end of the day, this is all about people! Let's walk in abundance so we can reach people.

Declare who God says you are today!

God says my name is Well-Supplied

My cup runs over

I always have more than enough and plenty to give

The Lord blesses me to be a blessing

Today's Prayer:

Heavenly Father,

Help me to see the true purpose of being well-supplied financially. As I attain it, help me to manage and use it in a way to honor You. Since I desire to further Your Kingdom and Your agenda on Earth, I am asking You to help me acquire wealth to be a Kingdom Financier for all You are doing. I ask for business ideas and concepts today. I ask according to Mark 11:24 and I believe I receive those ideas and concepts. Thank You for showing me how to acquire wealth and thank You for helping me manage it in a Godly manner.

Amen.

Cleansed

"But you were cleansed; you were made holy; you were made right with God by calling on the name of the Lord Jesus Christ and by the Spirit of our God."

-    1 Corinthians 6:11b NLT

"The Son radiates God's own glory and expresses the very character of God, and he sustains everything by the mighty power of his command. When he had cleansed us from our sins, he sat down in the place of honor at the right hand of the majestic God in heaven."

-    Hebrews 1:3 NLT

Did you know that God desires to have you come to Him boldly? Do you know why you can come boldly to Him? It is because you are completely cleansed! He sees no flaws.

Let me show you how God wants you to come to Him now that you are clean.

When I go and visit my parents' house, guess what? I often don't ask to come over. I go to the garage door, type in the password, and walk right in. There are times I will go straight to the kitchen and pour myself a glass of water. I do not go to the front door on my hands and knees, knock on the door, and beg my parents to come in. When I go into the kitchen I do not have to have tears in my eyes and ask for my parents' permission to get a drink of water. I can have boldness entering into my parents' home. This is how God wants you to come to His throne, boldly.

Now, I want you to imagine you are out at a restaurant. A few tables over you see my wife, Analisa, and I out to dinner. When our waiter brings our food you can see that I ordered some french fries. All of a sudden you see my wife get out of her seat, get down on her knees, and with a tear in her eye say, "Dustin, could I please have a fry?" What would your opinion of me be? Pretty low.

Well, I can assure you this does not happen. I'm sure other men experience what I am about to say, but whenever I order french fries, somehow a hand (belonging to my wife) crosses to my side of the table and takes some of my fries... WITHOUT ASKING. This is what boldness looks like.

So, what is boldness? Many people confuse boldness and arrogance. They can look similar; however, they are different. Boldness is confidence in the character of someone else. Arrogance is confidence in yourself. My wife can boldly take a french fry from my plate because she knows my character. She knows I want her to have one just as much as she does. Analisa does not take a fry because she has been good, she takes them because she knows I am good to her.

God delights in your boldness towards Him. I know this sounds strange for many people because, through religion, we have been taught to come to God on our hands and knees. We have been taught to come as a beggar expecting nothing. This is not how God wants you to approach Him. Actually, when you refer to yourself as a beggar it is disrespectful to what God has done in you. He wants you to approach Him confidently.

Come to God EXPECTING! There is a difference between asking expectantly and asking to see if it happens. Many Christians ask to see if something happens, but God wants you to ask and expect it to come to pass. Look at it like this, when I am in the kitchen and my wife asks me for a glass of water, she isn't sitting and hoping that glass of water comes to her. No, she is sitting there very confidently, expecting a glass of water is coming.

You might be wondering, "Dustin, why are you talking about boldness, I thought today was cleansed?" I am glad you asked! The reason that you can have boldness towards God is because of what He has done in you because you are clean and pure in His eyes. The reason that I believe most people don't feel like they can be bold towards God is because they don't feel worthy. I prefer to say it like this, people feel dirty. When we feel dirty it makes us feel like we are on the outside looking in. Feeling dirty keeps us standing at a distance from God. This also causes us to ask in a way where we are asking with no confident expectation. There is no boldness because we don't feel good enough, we feel dirty.

Listen, I know you have made mistakes. You may feel dirty. You may be fighting to come to God because you don't feel like you deserve to be near Him and you know how much filth you have been through. But guess what?! God doesn't see you that way! God sees you as cleansed, spotless, and without blemish. How do I know? Look at our scriptures for today in 1 Corinthians 6:11b and Hebrews 1:3. Go back and look at them. Did you notice something? Neither of them is talking of a future cleansing, but they are both in the past tense. We read "You WERE cleansed" and "When He HAD cleansed." This has already been done!

Don't be moved by how you feel, how you look, or what the devil says about you. YOU ARE CLEANSED. You stand pure before God.

I walk confidently into my parent's home because they love me. Analisa confidently takes french fries off my plate because I love her. You can come boldly before your Father because He loves you.

Stop carrying your past with you. Being made clean is not a journey, it happens when you invite Jesus into your life. Sometimes it may take time before you see it with your eyes and it may take time before you feel it, but you were cleansed in God's eyes the moment you were born again.

You are clean, so come boldly to your Father!

Declare who God says you are today!

God says my name is Cleansed

I can be bold because I am clean

In Christ old things have passed away and I am new

I am spotless and pure

I have been made clean

Today's Prayer:

Heavenly Father,

Thank You for cleansing me. Thank You for setting me free. Thank You for washing me and making me right in Your eyes. Help me to see myself as You see me. From this day forward, I will choose to come to You confidently. I know that You want me to come to You with confidence in Your character and since I have been made perfect in Your eyes, I know that I can.

Amen.

DAY 30

Hello, God says my name is

Redeemed

"Christ redeemed us from the curse of the law by becoming a curse for us—for it is written, 'Cursed is everyone who is hanged on a tree.'"

-      Galatians 3:13 ESV

"But when the fullness of time had come, God sent forth his Son, born of woman, born under the law, to redeem those who were under the law, so that we might receive adoption as sons."

-      Galatians 4:4-5 ESV

Let's start today with a story I heard several years ago, but sadly I don't remember where I heard it. There was a man that enjoyed being on the water. He was good at working with his hands so he decided to build a canoe. The man found the perfect tree, cut it down, and then spent months carving and perfecting his canoe. Once he was finished, he carved his initials into the side of the canoe and went to the local river. For years this man enjoyed his canoe, it was his prized possession and he took care of it like one. One day when he was on the river bank, he forgot to tie his canoe up and before he noticed, the canoe had drifted out of sight. The man was extremely disappointed because he lost his favorite possession.

Years later the man was in another town on business. As he walked by a small locally owned shop he noticed a beautiful canoe in the front window. When he went into the shop he noticed his initials carved into the side of the canoe. He found the owner and shared his story about the canoe, however, the owner said: "I am sorry to hear that, but it belongs to me now." The man opened his wallet, paid for the canoe, and went home full of joy that he once again had his canoe.

What do I want you to take from this? This is a picture of what it means to redeem something. Redeem means to buy back. It happens when a price is paid to recover something from the power of another. The canoe was lost to the shop owner so it had to be purchased to be brought back to the man who created it. The first man was responsible for the creation of the canoe because he was the one who made it, but it had been lost to the possession of someone else, so he had to pay a price to get it back.

Just like that canoe, we are God's creation but we were lost to the power of someone else. Sin caused us to be lost to another ruler, Satan.

You were created by God as the apple of His eye and His prized possession. When Adam and Eve chose to obey the devil in the Garden of Eden, mankind was brought under the power of the kingdom of darkness. We were born with a sinful nature that came from our original parents, Adam and Eve. This sinful nature placed us under the power of Satan. A price was then required to buy us back from the power of darkness, even though we were God's creation. This price was Jesus Christ taking on your sin and the curse that came from our sin. When Jesus paid it we were no longer responsible for the payment.

The Bible says "Christ redeemed us from the curse of the law by becoming a curse for us—for it is written, 'Cursed is everyone who is hanged on a tree'" in Galatians 3:13 ESV. And then in Galatians 4:4-5 ESV we find this, "But when the fullness of time had come, God sent forth his Son, born of woman, born under the law, to redeem those who were under the law, so that we might receive adoption as sons."

We were under a curse because of our sin and had no way to buy ourselves out from under that curse. The Bible says that Jesus redeemed us by becoming a curse for us. In other words, He paid for the sin and the curse so that you no longer were responsible for the bill.

The canoe couldn't pay for itself to get out and neither could we. Someone else had to do it.

You are Redeemed. God says you have been redeemed, you have been bought back. Although you were once in darkness, you have been delivered from the power of darkness and translated into God's Kingdom (Colossians 1:13). You have been purchased out from under Satan's power and his dominion that he claims over you. This has already taken place. This is not a future event. You will not be redeemed when you go to Heaven. You will not be redeemed when Satan is gone forever. You are redeemed now. Satan no longer has power over you.

Just like the canoe was in the hands of the shop owner, we were once under the power of the god of this world, the devil.

Jesus paid the price for you. When you said yes to Him; Jesus walked you out of the devil's shop and out from under his dominion. Satan has nothing on you anymore.

In Psalm 107:2 we find the following "Let the redeemed of the Lord say so." God is telling those that are redeemed to remind the enemy they are redeemed. He is saying to remind the enemy that he no longer has a hold on you. Let others know you are redeemed and that they don't have to live in bondage any longer.

We are supposed to speak and declare what God has done.

We are redeemed!

Declare who God says you are today!

God says my name is Redeemed

I am purchased

Jesus has set me free

I am no longer under Satan's power

I am redeemed so I will say so

Today's Prayer:

Heavenly Father,

Thank You for redeeming me. Thank You for paying the price that I never could, by sending Your Son to purchase me back from the power of darkness. I ask that You would continue to open my eyes to all that You have redeemed me from. I believe that I am no longer under Satan's dominion, so give me wisdom and discernment to identify Satan's schemes against me in his attempt to keep me in bondage. I choose to believe that I have been redeemed from the curse of the law and everything that results from sin.

Amen.

Believer

"For God so loved the world that he gave his one and only Son, that whoever believes in him shall not perish but have eternal life.

-     John 3:16 NIV

"All things are possible for one who believes."

-     Mark 9:23b ESV

Well, here we are my friend, day thirty-one. I hope that these thirty-one days have opened your eyes to who you truly are. I pray that you continue to use this devotional as a resource and continually allow yourself to be reminded who you are in God's eyes. Remember, faith comes by hearing, so it's good to keep hearing and hearing and hearing (Romans 10:17).

Allow me to ask you a quick question. What is a Believer? Quite simply, a Believer is someone who believes. The moment you called upon the name of Jesus and decided to put your faith in Him for your salvation, you became a Believer. Now, as a Believer, when God looks at you He sees a mountain mover. Yes, you! Don't feel like a mountain mover? That doesn't matter.

Check out Mark 11:23 in the NIV where we read, "Truly I tell you, if anyone says to this mountain, 'Go, throw yourself into the sea,' and does not doubt in their heart but believes that what they say will happen, it will be done for them." Jesus was speaking here and He said that if anyone says this to the mountain, doesn't doubt, and <u>believes</u> it will happen, then the mountain <u>will</u> move. So, remind me, what does a Believer do? They believe. What does a doubter do? They doubt, and you are not a doubter. God sees you as a Believer, and since a Believer can move mountains, that would make you a mountain-mover.

"But, Dustin, God is the mountain-mover, not me." Well, yes and no. Check out what Paul said in 1 Corinthians 13:2. He said, "If I had such faith that I could move mountains." Please notice, Paul did not say, "If I had faith that God could move the mountains for me." Paul, inspired by the Holy Spirit, wrote those words. When Paul said "I could move mountains," he was insinuating that he could do it. The reason he said this was because he knew that God was on the inside of him and he understood that God works through us. You see, God has made you much bigger and more powerful than you realize.

I want to be very clear. Without God, we can do nothing. But thank God, we aren't without Him. He is with us 24/7 and He has told us to speak to the mountain and it would move. God has told us to bind and loose things on Earth and then Heaven would back us up (Matthew 18:18). God wants to partner with us as His vessels in the Earth.

So, what does this partnership with God look like?

READ THE FOLLOWING CAREFULLY!

Here is an illustration for you. Let's say you have a big pile of dirt in your yard. However, you do not know how to move it and you also don't have the tools to move it. Well, you know that I am an 'expert dirt-pile-mover," so you give me a call. I come over to your house and pull into your driveway with my truck full of tools. When I get there you ask for my help and you ask me how to move it. I then give you access to all the tools you need to move it and I even tell you exactly how to make it happen. You then take the tools I gave you and the knowledge I shared and proceeded to move the dirt.

Now, here is a question! Who moved the dirt? Well, you did with my help. You could not have done it without wisdom from me and access to my tools.

Friend, this is how it is with us and God. This is how God helps us with the mountains in our life. God partners with you to accomplish His will on the Earth. Without God, we don't have the wisdom to do anything on the Earth. Without God, we don't have the tools or the power to move the mountains. But, thank God, we are not without Him!

God gives us access to His wisdom and His tools.

All things are possible with God (Mark 10:27), but all things are also possible for a Believer (Mark 9:23). You are a Believer and all things are possible for you! With God in your corner, you have access to everything you need. God said He would never leave you or forsake you (Hebrews 13:5). He is always right there to tell you what to do and how to do it.

Sometimes, when we walk through dark places in life we need to be reminded of one simple statement by Jesus, "do not be afraid, only believe" (Mark 5:36b). ONLY BELIEVE. In other words, be a believer, act like you're supposed to, and believe. Refuse to doubt. Refuse to fear. When fear talks about all those bad things that could happen, remind fear that ALL THINGS are possible to a believer.

Remember that God is with you and a believer can move mountains.

As you finish reading today, let God expand the vision of who and what you truly are. Let it become real inside of you. God has made you into a powerful, wonderful, and amazing creature and nothing in the world can stand in your way.

God is with you!

Greater is He that is inside of you, than he that is in the world!

God is for you so nothing can stand against you!

You can speak to the mountain and see it move.

(1 John 4:4, Romans 8:31, & Mark 11:23)

Declare who God says you are today!

God says my name is Believer

I am a mountain-mover

Greater is He that is on the inside of me

All things are possible to me

God is on my side

Today's Prayer:

Heavenly Father,

Today, I pray this genuine prayer out of my heart. Show me just how powerful You have made me in Christ. Help me as I venture to remove all doubt and unbelief from my life. You said that I would move mountains and You said that all things are possible to me as a believer, so help me see what this means. I know that I am nothing without You, but thank God, I am not without You, so I am not nothing! I am a child of God who was created to take territory from the kingdom of darkness here on the Earth.

Amen.

Thank you for reading!

If you enjoyed reading this book and are interested in staying connected with us further I want to invite you to find us on social media. PLEASE take a moment and share with us how God spoke to you as you read these pages.

There have been many times in my life where I felt God strongly impress upon me the word MEDIA. It was almost like the word burned in my spirit. I know that God has called Analisa and myself to do ministry uniquely through media channels. Our YouTube channel is designed to bring you simple and high-quality teaching that helps you see who God is and who God says you are.

We obviously love people and have a passion for face-to-face ministry but there is something powerful about using media to amplify the message of Jesus Christ.

You are who He says you are,

Dustin Barker

For more resources, please take a moment to connect with us:

YouTube   channel URL youtube.com/dustinbarker

Instagram   @dustin.barker

Facebook   facebook.com/thedustinbarker

Printed in Dunstable, United Kingdom